From Despair to Hope and Back

From
DESPAIR
to
HOPE
and
BACK

yehudit feuer

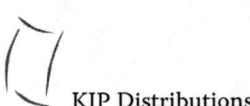
KIP Distributions

From Despair To Hope And Back
by Yehudit Feuer

Copyright © 2015 Yehudit Feuer

All rights reserved

No part of this book may be used or reproduced in any manner whatsoever without written permission from the copyright owner, except in the case of brief quotations embodied in reviews and articles.

Cover design by Yehudit Feuer

Typeset by Ariel Walden

Printed in Israel

First Edition

ISBN 978-965-7589-14-4

"Thou shalt not be a victim,

thou shalt not be a perpetrator,

but thou shalt never be a bystander."

Victor Emil Frankl

*I*n memory of my grandparents

Gizella and Yitzhak Feuer

whose lives were terminated

one day in May, 1944.

CONTENTS

Preface: Joel E. Dimsdale, M.D.   11

Introduction: Yehudit Feldmann-Feuer   13

DESPAIR

1. 2012: Celebrating 60 Years of a Historic Agreement   19
2. 1945 Awakening from a Nightmare   24
3. An experiment in Human Resilience   32

HOPE

4. Spotlight on the Holocaust and its Survivors   40
5. The Exclusive "Holocaust Survivors' Club"   45
6. The Survivors' Choice: Never Again!   52
7. Zionist Anyone?   55
8. To The Promised Land – a Home Coming   61
9. The Fighters for Independence   66
10. "The Survivor Syndrome"   69
11. We Are All Equals, Except . . .   71
12. Communal Farms: A New Wave of Startups   73

DESPAIR

13.	Germany Offers – Israel Accepts	76
14.	A Kind of Partnership	84
15.	The Eichmann Trial	88
16.	Life in Two Parallel Social Universes	92
17.	Election Upheaval 18th	96
18.	Living with Post Trauma – Post *WHAT??*	99
19.	A Matter of Phrasing	104
20.	Even More Holocaust Assets Available!	106
21.	Hospitalized, Half a Century Later	110
22.	Negotiations & Negotiators	114
23.	". . . But What About the Individuals?" – Who are those Individuals?	118
24.	Making "Historic and Social Justice" – Indeed!?	125
25.	"We Won't Forget"	127
26.	The Problem with Helping our Survivors	132
27.	Our Selective Memory of the Shoah	138
28.	A Part of Our Legacy	141

PREFACE

"Survivors of Nazi death camps have been called *'collectors of justice.'* They seek something beyond economic or social restitution. They seek something closer to acknowledgement of crimes committed against them and punishment of those responsible in order to *re-establish at least the semblance of a moral universe.* The impulse to bear witness, beginning with a sense of responsibility to the dead, can readily extend into a mission. For many survivors, the mission took the form of involvement in the creation of the State of Israel."

—Joel E. Dimsdale, M.D.

INTRODUCTION:
YEHUDIT FELDMANN-FEUER

I spent the first four years of my life in Satu-Mare[1] in a loving extended family, headed by my grandfather, Yitzhak Feuer.

I enjoyed watching the fascinating social behavior of ants in our courtyard, and, as the only granddaughter in the household, I had the privilege of tasting the first strawberries of the season in our vegetable garden, and to hide the afikoman[2] on the eve of Passover. But above all, I loved to sit on my beloved granddaddy's lap, while he drew horses for me on the margins of his newspaper.

We changed our tranquil life with my grandparents in favor of Hungary's Capital, Budapest, a lively, noisy big city, where life was full of excitement and adventures.

In spring, 1944, I was told that I didn't have to go back to school to finish 2nd grade. To be honest, I didn't mind very much for I never liked being in the frame of any formal education. Besides, I already knew how to read and write, so I felt sure that equipped with those skills, I would be able to fulfill all of my ambitions in life.

Right after that interrupted school year, there came many other

---

1. Satu-Mare: a town in Transylvania, which was Hungary before WWII but now belongs to Rumania.
2. "afikoman" – a piece broken off from a matzo during a Seder and put aside to be eaten at the end of the meal. It is traditionally hidden during the Seder to be searched for by the children present.

With my cousin, Shmilu, who was my best friend, until he disappeared from my life when we were both 8 years old

Strolling with my mom, Blanka, and aunt Sara who "didn't come back..."

changes in our daily routine: one day, all my clothes were decorated with a Star-of-David shaped yellow badge; next, we left our flat in the neighborhood of Buda and moved in with a woman called Mrs. Farkas in another neighborhood, called "Ghetto Budapest", where all our neighbors were Jewish. Here, my mother prepared a rucksack with cans, toilet articles and warm clothes, something that created a sense of some temporary living arrangement – perhaps signaling additional changes to come?

One day we prepared for an excursion with all the tenants of our neighborhood invited; we spent all the day in a huge field, and slept at night in the open-air. The next morning, my mom took a can with liver paste out of her rucksack, which tasted very good, and that same evening we all returned to the ghetto. I thought it was a nice picnic, but most of the grownups didn't seem to have enjoyed it.

... A few years later, I found out that the "picnic outing" had been planned to continue as a "train ride" to Auschwitz, but that plan failed to materialize, because the railroad tracks had been bombarded by the Allied Forces.

With the autumn clouds of 1944, another new chapter opened in my life. After the plan to load the Jews in Budapest on a train had failed, Adolf Eichmann prepared an alternative plan toward "The Final Solution."

In order to reduce the number of train passengers to just the children and the elderly among us, he made the rest of the grownups walk to concentration camps in Poland and Germany.

Adolf Eichmann in SS uniform

One morning two gendarmes showed up in our flat, ordered us to go down to the street, and from there, everything proceeded very quickly. This time, my mother took out a pair of scissors from her rucksack, cut off my braids, which she put inside her rucksack, and told me: "Be a good girl, and I will come back." After that she climbed up on the truck parked nearby, filled with other grownups, all assigned to walk to Bergen Belsen.

After the truck disappeared from the horizon, I remained standing on the street for some time, determined to be a very good girl.

❊❊❊

I was a good girl, as I had promised, and my mother came back, as she had promised.

– About the long, bumpy two-year journey from our separation to our reunion, I may sometime write another book or two. But for now, I intend only to reflect on some of my impressions of the socio-political trends that have shaped Israel's society in general and its Holocaust survivors in particular since I made Aliyah about 60 years ago.

❊❊❊

I had the privilege to spend my teen-years in Sweden – a country that was at the time "the envy of the world". The Swedish people were generous enough to receive a large group of seriously diseased, traumatized Holocaust survivors, right after liberation from the Nazi concentration camps.

Graduating from high school, celebrating with my young, blond neighbors.

In Sweden, Freedom and Silence are of supreme values, even praised in its national anthem. Its population has created a unique quality of life in an aesthetic environment, perhaps inspired by the breath-taking views with which it is blessed.

One day I went to the Jewish community center in our city where they showed a film from Israel; young men and women in shorts and "kova tembel" (Israeli "national hat"), working in the field in scorching heat, apparently all cheerful, which comes naturally with constructive work and the joy of creation, typical for young idealists, builders of a new country. My brain became infected with the bug of Zionism and from that moment on, I didn't stop dreaming of the day when I would join the young pioneers, the builders of the new Jewish State.

In December 1954 I was at last sailing on my way to Israel. In Sweden it was already snowing, but all along the Mediterranean Sea the sun was shining generously all day long, and the night sky was covered with a crowd of shimmering stars, as some of the special treats on our way to the Holy Land.

On the ship I met a young man who reminded me of a prince from the Arabian Nights. He explained that he comes from a Yemenite family in Israel. He taught me to count from one to five in Hebrew, and insisted on pronouncing the sound "khet" correctly at the beginning of "khamesh" (five).

After arriving in Israel, I learned another thousand Hebrew words at an "ulpan," this time in a kibbutz, together with other newcomers from Persia, Belgium, Egypt, the US, and Morocco. At the same time, I also learned to plant Eucalyptus trees in the fields, to wash a couple of hundred dishes in the dining hall, and some great Israeli folk dances.

However, I was also surprised to find out that even among the kibbutz members not everybody enjoyed total equality.

During my first visits to Tel Aviv, I was amazed by the colorful population of our small homeland. The overloaded shabby buses were a part of the local exotic view, and I regarded the amorphous shapes of the congested queues to the buses as an expression of the Middle Eastern temperament.

After some time, my romantic attitude towards such phenomena in our region has changed a lot.

※※※

Two years of military service were some of the most significant among a whole series of adventures in my youth. There, I had the honor to know some of the most prominent national heroes of that period in our history: Arik Sharon, "Raful"/Rafael Eitan, Meir Har Zion, and other exceptional role models, some of whom didn't return from the battle fields.

By the end of my service, it was time to decide whether to go back to Sweden or to stay.

The choice was between good old peaceful, well organized Sweden with one of the highest standards of living in the world, versus a newly established poor country, still fighting for its very existence, in the hands of some inexperienced leaders. – However, all those difficulties were about to change soon, after, as stated in the Proclamation of Israel's Independence:

In Kibutz Ein Hashofet, where I learned both Hebrew and to work in the fields.

"Lone soldier" paratrooper; my mom on visit in Israel, asking: So, when are you coming home?

> The State of Israel will be open for Jewish immigration and the ingathering of the exiles . . . it will be

based on freedom, justice, and peace as envisaged by the prophets of Israel; it will ensure complete equality of social and political rights to all its inhabitants, irrespective of religion, race or sex . . .

Who could resist the unique opportunity to help build such an exemplary society in the Jewish Homeland?
    I couldn't.

Israel Declaration of Independence

1 2012: CELEBRATING 60 YEARS OF A HISTORIC AGREEMENT

"There Is No Business Like Shoah Business"

It was Abba Eban, former Israeli foreign minister, who came up with the slogan above, alluding to huge profits made by the cynical use of one of the greatest man-made disasters in history:

> The mass murder of Jews under the German Nazi regime during the period 1941–5. More than 6 million European Jews, as well as members of other persecuted groups, were murdered at concentration camps such as Auschwitz.[1]

"Memory industry" is another slanderous label for the trade that grew out of the genuine effort to commemorate the Holocaust. It stands for the prosperous commerce, dealing with books, films, memorabilia, etc., more or less linked to the Holocaust, while "Shoah business" refers to the exploitation of human suffering and loss during the Nazi regime by politicians, administrators, attorneys, and various organizations, to mention just a few of the more or less high ranking public activists and actions involved in the "business".

---

1. Oxford Dictionaries, Language matters.

"Money makes the world go round" is also the central theme in the musical Cabaret,[2] to illustrate that currency plays a very important role in our world, given its close association with Power.

Money, according to Wikipedia, is

> any item or verifiable record that is generally accepted as payment for goods and services and repayment of debts in a particular country or socio-economic context

while Debt, in turn, is described as

> an obligation owed by one party (the debtor) to a second party, the creditor; the term can also be used metaphorically to cover moral obligations and other interactions not based on economic value . . . Some companies and corporations use debt as a part of their overall corporate finance strategy.

Paying compensation to victims of the Holocaust falls into the category of the moral obligation that Germany was compelled to fulfill after its defeat in WWII, so that the victorious Allied Forces would agree to recognize the German Federal Republic as a sovereign state.

Hence, in September 1951, Chancellor Konrad Adenauer delivered a formal message, admitting to the *"unspeakable crimes"* that were committed in the name of the German people, which called for the solution to "the material indemnity problem". That solution led to the Reparations Agreement,[3] a.k.a. The Luxembourg Agreement, which was signed in 1952 by the West German and Israeli governments, and the "Claims Conference".

The implementation of paying material indemnity behooved the need to convert "infinite suffering" into cash, i.e., money made available to the holocaust victims; of course, that kind of conversion called for professional expertise – jobs that became soon filled by experts, all eager to serve the victims in question, by mediating between the individuals who have survived those "unspeakable crimes" committed

---

2. Cabaret – musical based on a book by Christopher Isherwood, music by John Kander and lyrics by Fred Ebb.
3. From: Reparations Agreement between Israel and West Germany, Wikipedia.

CELEBRATING 60 YEARS OF A HISTORIC AGREEMENT 21

Konrad Adenauer

during the Nazi regime – in this case "the creditors" – and Germany, i.e., "the moral debtor".

Sixty years later, the survivors' various expert representatives looked back at their achievements as mediators with great satisfaction.

In July 2012, the U.S. Holocaust Memorial Museum in Washington hosted a group of such mediators from the U.S., Germany, and Israel. They all came to celebrate the 60th anniversary of the Reparations Agreement that led to some of their most lucrative mediating jobs in the course of the past six decades.

Dr. Michael Pinto-Duschinsky,[4] a British honorary academic advisor to the London-based Claims for Jewish Slave Labor Compensation and a Holocaust survivor himself, who attended the meeting in Washington, describes the attitude of the mediators as "an exercise in self-congratulation".

In his role as honorary advisor to former slave laborers in London during talks in the 1990s, Dr. Duschinsky became closely familiar with ways in which mediators handled cases of slave labor survivors

---

4. Dr. Michael Pinto-Duschinsky is "a British political scientist who was appointed in 2011 by Prime Minister David Cameron to the UK Commission on a Bill of Rights. A Holocaust survivor, he was honorary academic advisor to the London-based Claims for Jewish Slave Labor Compensation." In the Jewish Ideas Daily.

and the experts who represented the victims' claims to German compensation.

In his article "Holocaust Reparations: The Back Story",[5] Dr. Duschinsky recounts some of the procedures to which slave labor survivors repeatedly fell prey; schemes concocted by the negotiators vis a vis Germany while dealing with "unspeakable crimes" of the Nazis – crimes that just a few decades earlier The Federal Government declared as "a moral and material indemnity problem", which it was prepared to solve "... *thus easing the way to the spiritual settlement of infinite suffering.* "

In Dr Duschinsky's "The Back Story", we learn about lawyers who took multi-million dollar wages for themselves, while settling for fractions out of their own rewards for their clients, the Holocaust survivors – experts who were hired to find solution to the moral and material indemnity for Nazi victims' infinite suffering, in the words of Chancellor Adenauer.

In one notable example, the delegate Stuart Eizenstat – a prominent Jewish corporate lawyer – reasoned that it was better for elderly survivors to settle out of court rather than pursuing lawsuits.

Why? – Because in that way, argued Mr. Eizenstat, former slave laborers would have a chance to get some money out of the several billion dollars that Germany has pledged, before they died, while lawsuits sometimes risk to be lost, or dragged out in time until the victims were no longer alive.

Eizenstat, who at some point received the "Great Negotiator" award from Harvard Law School, held a festive speech at the celebration in Washington, including the statement:

> the Claims Conference vision, we hope, of meaningful compensation and reparations during the last 60 years has truly brought a reconciliation between Germany, the Jewish people, and the state of Israel.

As to The Claims Conference, it was charged with embezzling 57 million US dollars in one of the series of its financial scandals since the organization was established. In 2006, The London Jewish

---

5. Holocaust Reparations: The Back Story By Michael Pinto-Duschinsky, Jewish Ideas Daily, August 13, 2012

Chronicle revealed that the chief official of the Claims Conference earned 437,811 US dollars a year, while forced laborers – which is the softened term that the Germans prefer to use instead of wartime slaves – received $7,500, and at the same time required to give up all further legal rights, i.e.: no admission to legal liability for the atrocities of the Nazi "Death through Work" program.

Isi Leibler wrote in his article "No end to Claims Conference distortions and shamelessness":

> The mishandling of sacred Holocaust restitution funds represents the greatest moral failure of organized Jewish life in our generation.[6]

And just in case some negotiator would have any qualms about earning fortunes on account of those who survived the "unspeakable crimes" of the Holocaust – note a seasoned psychiatrist's assertion that

> **It was better that the survivors should die happy rather than be told that they were receiving a raw deal.**

---

6. Isi Leibler, the Jerusalem Post, 21.10. 2013

2 1945 – AWAKENING FROM A NIGHTMARE

In spring 1945, once Germany was defeated, the Allied Forces[1] liberated the last survivors of the concentration camps in Poland, Germany, and Austria.

That ended the wave of mass murder that swept across Europe in the frame of "the final solution"[2] of the Nazi regime, which came to be known as the Shoah.[3]

The liberated inmates of the death camps were slowly awakening from the nightmare of starvation, torture, or the threat of being beaten to death any moment.

They appeared like moving skeletons, indistinguishable one from another. They seemed to have preserved some of their basic instincts: they could still feel hunger and pain, but were mentally confused and

---

1. In World War II the chief Allied Powers were Great Britain, France (except during the German occupation, 1940–44), the Soviet Union (after its entry in June 1941, the United States (after its entry on Dec. 8–11, 1941 and China. Encyclopædia Britannica, Inc.
2. The Nazis frequently used euphemistic language to disguise the true nature of their crimes. They used the term "Final Solution" to refer to their plan to annihilate the Jewish people. © United States Holocaust Memorial Museum, Washington, DC.
3. "Beginning in March 1942, . . . 4,500,000 human beings were massacred. By the end of World War II the toll had risen to approximately 6,000,000 Jews, including 1,500,000 children, who perished at the hands of the Nazi murderers." From: Survivor Stories

Germany, 1945, Camp prisoners waving to their liberators Credit: Yad Vashem

Dachau, Germany, 1945, A survivor sitting on a bag. Yad Vashem

Bergen-Belsen, 1945, survivors after liberation Credit: Yad Vashem

Bergen-Belsen, 1945, survivors after liberation Credit: Yad Vashem

*Bergen Belsen, Germany, 1945, A woman infected with typhus
Credit: Yad Vashem*

disoriented, and, thankfully, emotionally numb, apparently indifferent to the heaps of corpses that kept growing before their eyes.

> Men and women clad in rags and barely able to move from starvation and typhus lay in their straw bunks in every state of filth and degradation. The dead and dying could not be distinguished. Men and women collapsed as they walked and fell dead.[4]

Eventually, though, the survivors began to slowly return to what resembled their former physical features; they made a significant step toward normalcy when they began to recognize each other, not only by the slave number tattooed on their forearms, but by their personal characteristic features, and to call each other by their names.

---

4. The Holocaust – Research Papers, twagzz.

AUSCHWITZ: "GATE TO HELL"

Birkenau, Poland, An elderly Jewish woman supervising young children on their way to the gas chambers. Credit: Yad Vashem

Auschwitz concentration camp was a network of German Nazi concentration camps and extermination camps built and operated by the Third Reich in Polish areas annexed by Nazi Germany during World War II. It consisted of *Auschwitz I* (the original camp), *Auschwitz II–Birkenau* (a combination concentration / extermination camp), *Auschwitz III*–Monowitz (a labor camp to staff an IG Farben factory), and 45 satellite camps.[1]

---

1. Auschwitz concentration camp. Wikipedia, the free encyclopedia

AUSCHWITZ: "GATE TO HELL"

Birkenau, Poland, Jews on the platform, after arriving from a train 27/5/1944 Credit: Yad Vashem

Auschwitz I was first constructed to hold Polish political prisoners, who began to arrive in May 1940. The first extermination of prisoners took place in September 1941, and *Auschwitz II–Birkenau* went on to become a major site of the Nazi "Final Solution to the Jewish question. From early 1942 until late 1944, transport trains delivered Jews to the camp's gas chambers from all over German-occupied Europe, where they were killed with the pesticide Zyklon B.[2]

At least 1.1 million prisoners died at Auschwitz, around 90 percent of them Jewish; approximately 1 in 6 Jews killed in the Holocaust died at the camp. Others deported to Auschwitz included 150,000 Poles, 23,000 Romani and Sinti, 15,000 Soviet prisoners of war, 400 Jehovah's Witnesses, homosexuals, and tens of thousands of people of diverse nationalities. Living conditions were brutal, and many of those not killed in the gas chambers died of starvation, forced labor, infectious diseases, individual executions, and medical experiments.[3]

---

2. Auschwitz concentration camp. Wikipedia, the free encyclopedia
3. Auschwitz concentration camp. Wikipedia, the free encyclopedia

Jews undergoing selection on the ramp - death to the left, life to the right. Credit: Yad Vashem

Children were waved to the left hand side – death Credit: Yad Vashem

Elderly men and women, selected for death, waiting on the ramp before being taken to the gas chamber. Credit: Yad Vashem

3 AN EXPERIMENT IN HUMAN RESILIENCE

Hungarian Jews are forced to move to ghetto areas Credit: Yad Vashem

The Implementation of the Final Solution

With the advent of the European-wide *Final Solution* the Jews were generally ordered to gather within close proximity of railroad stations. They were then deported to the extermination camps on extended trips under horrendous conditions that claimed many victims. The Jews of Europe were systematically murdered in the extermination camps as part of the Final Solution. In some of the

Warsaw, Poland, Deportation of Jews to the ghetto Credit: Yad Vashem

Jews captured during the suppression of the Warsaw Ghetto Uprising Credit: Yad Vashem

A policeman forcing Jews to bathe in sewage Credit: Yad Vashem

camps permanent gas chambers were erected. In Belzec, Sobibor, Treblinka and Chelmno, practically all of the deportees – men, women and children – were sent straight to their deaths.[1]

It is estimated that about 40,000 eastern European children were brought to Germany during the so called 'Heuaktion', the cover name used for the kidnapping children aged 10 to 14 who were considered suitable for "re-Germanization" into the Reich – one of several such operations carried out by the SS. 'Re-Germanization' was the process whereby 'racially desirable' individuals from the occupied territories by the Wehrmacht could become suitably educated for becoming citizens and part of the German people.[2]

Most of the Jews of Europe were dead by 1945. A civilization that had flourished for almost 2,000 years was no more.

The survivors – one from a town, two from a host – dazed, emaciated, bereaved beyond measure, gathered the remnants of

---

1. In: "The Holocaust" Credit: Yad Vashem
2. Source: United States Holocaust Memorial Museum

Auschwitz, Poland, July 1944, Polish children, before being transported to Germany for the "Heuaktion". United States Holocaust Memorial Museum

their vitality and the remaining sparks of their humanity, and rebuilt. They never meted out justice to their tormentors – for what justice could ever be achieved after such a crime? Rather, they turned to rebuilding: new families forever under the shadow of those absent; new life stories, forever warped by the wounds; new communities, forever haunted by the loss.

Warsaw, Poland, Starving children in the ghetto Credit: Yad Vashem

Bergen Belsen, Germany, A survivor, after the liberation. Credit: Yad Vashem

Auschwitz, Poland, A group of children after the liberation, 1945. Credit: Yad Vashem

Even after the survivors had no longer to starve, to freeze, or fear to be tortured, there were still about 200–300 Jews who continued to die from the damages of starvation, various illnesses and of the poisoned food that the Germans had left behind before escaping from the approaching Allied Forces.

Many of them fell into despair while witnessing the horror scenes of the ever growing heaps of corpses dragged away from the camps.

When they began to recover, started to heal physically, mentally and emotionally, they slowly began to realize that they are free – at least ceased to be slaves – and that after all, they had some kind of future ahead; however, the marks they carried from famine, diseases and trauma would last for the rest of their lives.

During the slow process of rehabilitation, they also started to realize that their families had died, that most of their close relatives and friends were gone, and what used to be their homes had been destroyed or confiscated.

※※※

As a unique episode in human history, the Holocaust has been analyzed, studied, discussed, disputed, and debated ever since it ended.

The victims of the Nazi genocide were Jews, Gypsies, mentally or physically disabled persons, Soviet prisoners-of-war, along with several "other undesirables."

They came from 21 different countries, speaking different languages, and from a wide range of socio-economic backgrounds; all those differences disappeared however very quickly in the cattle carts of the trains heading to the concentration camps, where they all became just a bunch of semiconscious slaves.

Those who made it to liberation would change their status again – this time for the rest of their lives: affected by a special kind of carefully planned, systematic dehumanization, they all became members of a distinct group of people who identify themselves first and foremost as "Holocaust survivors."

Thus, the survivors of the Holocaust would forever be set apart from every other group of people in the world. Even without any recognizable features that could distinguish them from other groups of people, being a Holocaust Survivor means being profoundly different from all other individuals, for better or for worse.

AN EXPERIMENT IN HUMAN RESILIENCE

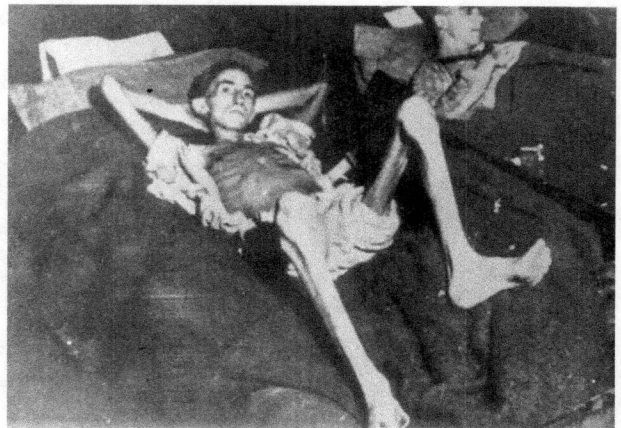

Auschwitz, Poland, Muselmanner, after the liberation. Credit: Yad Vashem

The source of this difference was graphically depicted by Yehiel Dinur[3] in his testimony at the Eichmann trial – a chronicle from the Planet Auschwitz:

Yehiel De-Nur testifies at the trial of Adolf Eichmann in 1961. Wikimedia Commons

> ... Time there was not as time is here on Planet Earth. Every split second on this planet followed a completely different clock. The residents of this planet had no names. They had no parents and no children. They did not go dressed as we do here. They were not born there and they did not give birth there. They did not live according to the laws of this world, nor did they die that way.

---

3. Yehiel De-Nur, Dinoor or Dinur, also known by his pen name Ka-Tsetnik 135633 ... was a Jewish writer and Holocaust survivor, whose books were inspired by his time as a prisoner in the Auschwitz concentration camp. From Wikipedia

4 SPOTLIGHT ON THE HOLOCAUST AND ITS SURVIVORS

In 1945, when Anglo-American and Soviet troops entered the concentration camps, they discovered piles of corpses, bones, and human ashes—testimony to Nazi mass murder. Soldiers also found thousands of survivors—Jews and non-Jews—suffering from starvation and disease.[1]

The Nazis left behind hundreds of thousands of concentration camp prisoners – displaced persons (DPs)[2] who had to be cared for, saved from further starvation, disease and death, and treated for various damages left from the infamous "Death Marches" at the hands of the Nazis.

"The same day I saw my first horror-camp, I visited every nook and cranny. I felt it my duty to be in a position from then on to testify about these things in case there ever grew up at home the belief or assumption that the stories of Nazi brutality were just propaganda."
General Dwight D. Eisenhower

---

1. The Aftermath of the Holocaust from: United States Holocaust Memorial Museum.
2. Displaced Persons and the Desire for a Jewish National Homeland, Dr Michael Brenner

General Dwight D Eisenhower Visits Atrocities Concentration Camp at Ohrdruf, Germany, April 12, 1945. Public Domain.

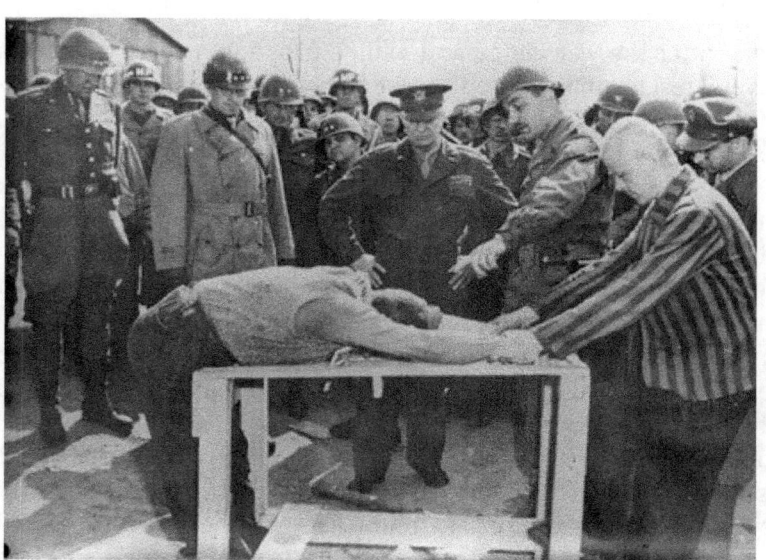

Buchenwald, Germany, Postwar, A demonstration of flogging for US army generals. The demonstration was done in front of Generals Patton, Bradley and Eisenhauer. Credit: Yad Vashem

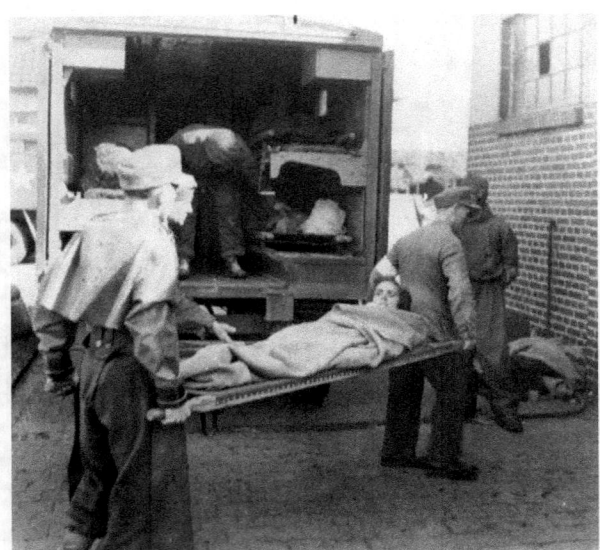

Bergen Belsen, Germany, Transferring survivors to a makeshift hospital at the time of liberation, 1945. Credit: Yad Vashem

Soon after the war ended and while Europe was still in total chaos, several rescue units arrived to care for the survivors. Eventually, some of these camps, the largest of them being Bergen Belsen, turned into temporary rehabilitation units.

The Allied powers tried to take on as much of this enormous mission of welfare as possible, but they had limited means for the task. The Allied Armies, the UNRA, the UN rehabilitation and support agency, were not prepared for the extensive rescue activities that were necessary, and they certainly were unable to provide the appropriate rehabilitation services that the survivors needed in their terrible condition. The food that was provided to the starved survivors was certainly generous and compassionate, but it was often too rich for their depleted systems, and tens of thousands more died as a result. Furthermore, the liberators didn't distinguish between Jewish survivors and other millions of prisoners and forced labor survivors, among whom were also Nazi collaborators, so initially, they all remained together in the same camps.

In any case, about 10 million displaced persons had to remain for

Buchenwald, Germany, Former inmates in their barracks after the liberation, 1945. Credit: Yad Vashem

Neubau, Austria, Survivors of Mauthausen at the 121st field army hospital, after the liberation. Credit: Yad Vashem

Journalists, accompanied by American military police, conduct an inspection tour of the newly liberated Buchenwald concentration camp. April 25, 1945, Buchenwald, Germany. Credit: National Archives and Records Administration, College Park Copyright: Public Domain

varying periods of time in the forced labor units and concentration/death camps even after liberation.

Many of the displaced persons were repatriated to their countries of origin within a short time, which eased some of the burden. However, most of the Jewish survivors refused to return to their former homes in Europe, where they had suffered fierce anti-Semitism and oppression both before and during the Holocaust. The majority of the Jewish survivors preferred therefore to remain in the German camps while waiting to be able to go either to Eretz Israel or to the United States – although that took often a long time to realize.

At the same time, those camps and their "residents" became major attractions to journalists, military staff, political delegates, and photographers from every corner of the world; some of their pictures and documentaries have since become familiar all over the world.

5 THE EXCLUSIVE "HOLOCAUST SURVIVORS' CLUB"

> Throughout history, sharing relationships have been a central mode of coping with and adapting to the environment. When the conditions of life are particularly harsh, making survival difficult, there is often an increase in reciprocal relationships.[1]

From the perspective of an outsider, the time the survivors had to remain in former death camps under such abnormal conditions seemed like a painful extension of their previous suffering as slaves; but for the survivors themselves, lingering in the camps meant spending more time in each other's company, was actually a blessing in disguise.

Later research found that victims of war, natural disasters and systematic persecution, who had a chance to remain in each other's company for some time, while sharing their common horrible experiences, were psychologically much better off than those who were separated from their groups soon after being traumatized.[2]

---

1. Source: Shamai Davidson, "Human Reciprocity Among The Jewish Prisoners In The Nazi Concentration Camps", The Nazi Concentration Camps, Yad Vashem 1984, pp. 555–572.
2. Peer Support/Peer Provided Services Underlying Processes, Benefits, and Critical Ingredients. Solomon, Phyllis Psychiatric Rehabilitation Journal, Vol 27(4), 2004, 392–401.

46   THE EXCLUSIVE "HOLOCAUST SURVIVORS' CLUB"

While lingering in the liberated concentration camps, the surviving "camp residents" organized their own exclusive "Holocaust Survivors' Club", based on a deep mutual understanding, grown out of their shared status as "Death Camp Graduates". They set up their own support groups, became each other's therapists and adopted each other as surrogate families.

Here, among themselves, they could express their pain, their wounded human dignity, outrage, hope, resignation; they had some time to grieve for all that they had lost: their marriage, children, parents, siblings, close families and friends, as well as their own lost childhood or youth.

Many did it in silence, trying to grasp the enormity of what they had endured, and the uncertainty about their future. Others sank back into hopelessness and deep depression, overwhelmed by the scenes of mountains of skeletons piled up on carts to be towed away.

Still others grieved while sobbing relentlessly:

- "On our way to the death camp, many of us died already inside of the cattle wagons; by the time our train reached its destinations, we all became mixed with the mass of rotten junk and our own stinking wastes..."

Jews from the Lodz ghetto are loaded onto freight trains for deportation to the Chelmno killing center. Lodz, Poland, between 1942 and 1944. — National Museum of American Jewish History, Philadelphia

Auschwitz, Poland: Hungarian Jews getting off a deportation train 1944. Credit: Yad Vashem

Selection of Hungarian Jews at the Auschwitz-Birkenau killing center. Credit: Yad Vashem

- Soon after we stumbled out of our wagon, we had to stand in a queue for inspection and SELECTION.
- My parents, my sister with her small children were shown to the left and I have never seen them again.

There were also some who have managed to preserve their humor and remembered scenes of horror with a smile:

- After we were stripped naked, they shaved our heads, so we couldn't recognize each other – which was funny, so we laughed . . .

Lubny, Ukraine, A mother with her two children assembled for mass execution, 16/10/1941 Credit: Yad Vashem

A few could joke about the drastic changes they went through:

- We had no problem choosing what to wear: in our barrack we were all clad in rags!

Nonetheless, the majority lamented most of the time:

- My sister with her baby and her three small children were all shown to the left . . . .

Then again –

- My younger sister was shown to the right, sentenced to take part in the meticulously planned "final solution" of the Fuhrer and his collaborates.

One girl remembered:

- The electric barbed wired fence served as an option to those of us who couldn't take it any longer. I often considered to follow their suite, but didn't have the courage to . . .

Women fit for work

Men fit for work. Women and men fit for work after the delousing process. The disinfection of those not selected for the gas chambers, and the shaving of their heads, was all part of the "registration" process at the camp. After they finished, they were given the prison uniforms. Credit: Yad Vashem

Auschwitz, Poland, Postwar, Barbed wire fences in the camp. Credit: Yad Vashem

While some were struggling to regain their sanity, listlessly, with eyes staring in the air, recalled . . . :

- Immediately after the train had stopped, the door of our wagon opened and we all poured out of the wagons; those of us who survived the thirst, hunger, stench, drenched in the soup of our own wastes. We emerged from our wagon without any trace of our former distinct individuality; we have all become a hoard of cattle within a few days.

There were those who would look for whatever good they could find in a situation that presented itself:

- I still remember the delicious pure air that I could inhale after the stench we were breathing inside the wagon during what appeared as an eternity.

or –

- We made sure to be tattooed by the person who had the neatest tattoo writing of all.

THE EXCLUSIVE "HOLOCAUST SURVIVORS' CLUB"   51

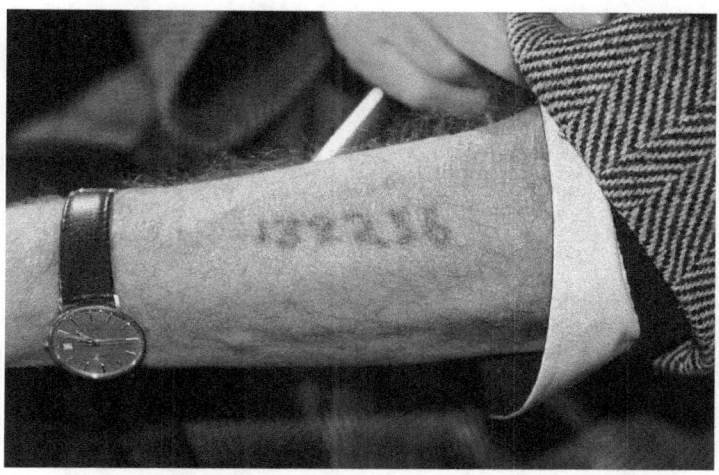

Long after the war, Auschwitz survivor Sam Rosenzweig displays his identification tattoo. Wikimedia Commons

Note: Identification of inmates in Nazi concentration camps was performed mostly with identification numbers marked on clothing, or later, tattooed on the skin.

Many of those "surrogate family adoptions" that were connected in their exclusive "Holocaust Survivors' Club" after liberation, lasted for a lifetime.

6 THE SURVIVORS' CHOICE – NEVER AGAIN![1]

The pain of forced exile from the homeland is deeply ingrained in the Jewish collective consciousness; deep, deep down, the Redemption of Israel has been the highest aspiration in the heart of every Jew in the Diaspora for at least the last 2,000 years. Jews who step for the first time on the soil of the independent State of Israel feel especially privileged for having achieved that aspiration. This was especially true for those who survived the hell of the Holocaust, and most especially for those among them who remembered praying with their family every year at Seder Pesach:

"Next year in Jerusalem!"

Waiting time in these transitory camps, which could last from a few months to years, were usually used constructively. Activities included

---

1. "'Never Again' Is Not Just a Slogan", the Algemeiner, March 15, 2011. Author: Dovid Efune: "Following the Holocaust, two phrases stand out above all others as concrete universal Jewish resolutions. The first, 'Zachor' (to remember), is to ensure that the past will never be forgotten and its memory will always serve as a guide for the future. The second, 'Never Again,' is not limited to the horrors of a particular time or place, nor by extent or methods, but rather it symbolizes the Jewish people's collective resolve to never stand by the blood of their brethren and to never allow innocents to be brutalized for the crime of being Jewish."

Old Temple of Jerusalem (by Dvr Tom Beazley) From Wikimedia Commons

Bratislava, Slovakia, A visit to a survivors' orphanage.
Credit: Yad Vashem Photographer: Arthur Zegart

education, culture, and some professional training courses.

The public activists and mentors represented a number of Jewish organizations that set up various improvised schools; in these teaching frames, the young survivors, most of whom were orphans, became exposed to their mentors' different worldviews and eventually most of them conformed to their ideologies. That is how sometimes children who were born in orthodox families, ended up as socialists and became ardent members of left-wing kibbutzim, while descendents of assimilated parents became devoted members of Orthodox, even Haredi communities.

> From time to time, my wife and daughter go for a walk around the block or for a drive to the store. I know they'll be back. But, watching my daughter wave bye-bye as they disappear around the corner of the house or up the street, I sometimes grieve for the murdered children of the Holocaust. They, too, had turned and waved, secure in that simple gesture and certain of their return.[2]

---

2. Unknown author from the webside: Welcome to my Journal

7 ZIONIST ANYONE?

Israel is often considered a live human laboratory that emerged amidst extraordinary social and political circumstances within a short period of time.

The pioneers, "chalutzim", of this country came in waves of immigrating Jews, flocking to The Old Homeland in order to escape persecution, degradation, and pogroms, which left them no hope for any viable future. Most of these pioneers were very young when they abandoned their ancestral homes – what Nicholas Christakis calls their "social universe"[1], according to which –

> Every choice you make, every behavior you exhibit, and even every desire you have, finds its roots in the social universe" of an individual.

However, contrary to *Christakis'* thesis, when our pioneers moved to Eretz Israel, they soon broke away from the orthodox traditions that used to dominate their social universe. They changed their world views based on newly adopted values, established new traditions; they distanced themselves from their cultural roots, created innovative,

---

[1]. "If You're So Free, Why Do You Follow Others? The Sociological Science Behind Social Networks and SocialInfluence." by Nicholas Christakis, Professor of Medical Sociology, Medicine, and Sociology at Harvard University

mostly secular lifestyles, which founded a new social universe that eventually shaped the special character of what is commonly considered the "typical Israeli".

Thus, in reality, our social imprints seem to work both ways. A recent example that demonstrates such a two-way influence is the new wave of Zionist immigrants, who are becoming acquainted with our local customs, get used to our particular social codes, etc. However, in the course of their absorption ("klita"), many of our new compatriots are also discovering certain practices which they refuse to accept, as they most certainly contradict the ideals of Zionism.

Ben Gurion visiting DP camps in Germany. Credit: Yad Vashem

One such practice is Israel's official attitude towards its Holocaust survivors.

**

There were several Jewish organizations who came to visit the newly liberated concentration camps, aiming to speak to the hearts and minds of the survivors there, but those who made the strongest impression on their audiences were the Zionist lobbyists:

They were organized, active and militant.[2]

When those activists arrived to the camps, they met the victims of the Holocaust when these were still freshly and unmistacably marked by:

---

2. The political lobby for a Jewish homeland in Palestine was greatly assisted by the demand and campaigning of the Jewish Displaced Persons in the DP camps at the end of World War II, particularly those at Bergen-Belsen. In "Displaced Persons and the Desire for a Jewish National Homeland", Dr Brenner discusses how circumstances connected the interests of the Zionists and the Jewish survivors and refugees.

Ben Gurion visiting DP camps in Germany. Credit: Yad Vashem

the intense, prolonged, repeated, cumulative, and unimaginably inhuman traumatic conditions on its victims.[3]

Yet, our visiting lobbyists didn't spare any effort to convince as many of the survivors as possible to make Aliyah; the Yishuv had to be reinforced by as many new immigrants as possible in the fight for Israel's independence, which meant: ousting the British and defending the borders of the future Jewish state from its Arab neighbors.

The strong, confident young men and women, who represented Eretz Israel, kept their public spellbound as they described the constructive, gratifying life of the pioneers back home. However, of all the arguments in favor of Eretz Israel, the strongest of them all was a future sovereign Israel that would offer the survivors of the Shoah

> . . . a life of dignity and equality for all its citizens.

Between the nightmares that usually tortured the freshly traumatized survivors in their sleep, the fervent speeches of the Zionist delegates would brighten up their waking hours, while day-dreaming of a life in gratification and self-realization in the "Land of Milk and Honey."

---

3. Jacob Lomranz: in: "The Skewed Image of the Holocaust Survivor and the Vicissitudes of Psychological Research"

Zeilsheim, Germany, Ben Gurion visiting the DP camp. Credit: Yad Vashem

One of the most passionate Zionists was Ben Gurion, who visited several DP camps in October 1945.

> To the people of the camp, he is God

wrote the American officer, Irving Heymont, about his visit in Landsberg.[4]

The passion of the visiting Zionists in the camps was highly contagious among the Jewish DPs, particularly in the camps in the three Western zones of Germany.

In a survey in April 1946, conducted by The Anglo-American Committee, 98% of them said they wanted to go to Eretz Israel, the Land of Israel, (which was usually called "Palestine" at that time). That, however, didn't necessarily reflect the true and honest desire of all of the respondents, for actually many of them preferred to emigrate elsewhere in the world; many of the pro-Palestine responses were rather a result of peer pressure, since Zionism was by far the most respected political ideal among the survivors – so much so that non-Zionists were at risk

---

4. Irving Heymont, 90, Commanded Displaced Persons Camp After WWII, Washington Post Staff Writer, April 8, 2009

of being unpopular, even socially ostracized; the Zionist residents of the camps were definitely on the top of the popularity scale.

Liberated but not free – that is the paradox of the Jew

Eventually, the Jewish survivors would have to leave the camps and they each had to find a place to start a new life. It was a fatal decision to make, while still feeling 'liberated but not free'[5] – and if *Nicholas Christakis*[6] is right, then the place they would chose would become their new "Social Universe" that would shape much of their future actions, influence their opinions, and ultimately affect their destiny.

The survivors' motto "never again" meant a life in reasonable safety.

However, for some, "safety" meant the Americas or other Western countries, known as politically stable with well established economies – although while choosing that option, they also remembered that in their countries of origin, similar favorable conditions have turned out to be disastrous for Jews, so . . .

For others, it meant first and foremost safety from further persecution and degradation, and that, in turn, signified a sovereign Jewish state, where they could realize their dream of a life amongst loyal, mutually supportive brethren. – Of course, such a state would still have to be fought for, in politically unstable and materially less than comfortable conditions, but that seemed like a challenge that they would be able to tackle in due time.

Ultimately, there were mainly three categories among the Jewish survivors who were looking for a place to start a new life:

- those who found family or friends in various parts of the world and chose to join them;
- those who went back to Europe, where they used to have a good

---

5. "Liberated but not free – that it is the Paradox of the Jew." Military Rabbi Abraham Klausner, Dachau, June 1945
6. "Every choice you make, every behavior you exhibit, and even every desire you have finds its roots in the social universe" in which an individual will spend his/her life." Nicholas Christakis, American physician and social scientist.

life as assimilated, loyal citizens in the Diaspora, before they were labeled as subhuman creatures and sent for extermination. Most of these were not Zionists, although after the Shoah, many of them did consider going to Eretz Israel as a viable option.
- Then, there were the Zionists, for whom this was a chance to realize their dream to settle in the ancient Jewish Homeland.

The latter group wanted to make Aliyah as soon as possible, although most of them had to wait until Israel became independent in May 1948, or were stopped on their way by the dictates of the British mandate.

Yet, about 480,000 Jews did manage to reach Palestine, legally or illegally, during the days of the Mandate, and by the declaration of the State of Israel, the Jewish population was about 650,000.[7]

The illegal immigration was nicknamed "Aliyah B," to differentiate it from the legally approved but very restricted immigration. It began after WWI and the establishment of the British Mandate with its immigration quotas.

The immigrants arrived by land and by sea, and from 1947 by air as well.

The illegal immigrant ship Exodus 1947

---

7. The Israel Ministry of Foreign Affairs

8 TO THE PROMISED LAND – A HOME COMING

According to psychiatrist, Prof. Joel Dimsdale, among the characteristics common to Holocaust survivors are:

> The impulse to bear witness, beginning with a sense of responsibility to the dead, can readily extend into a mission. For many survivors, the mission took the form of involvement in the creation of the State of Israel.[1]

The survivors who chose to "go to Palestine" of all other possibilities, didn't have any illusions about settling comfortably in an already well established country. They knew that in every wave of Aliyah,[2] a significant number of settlers gave up the struggle of building the Land and decided to settle elsewhere in the world. Still, our survivors thought they would be able to cope with wars, austerity, diseases, learning Hebrew, harsh climate, and several other challenges of the hour; they were hoping to capitalize on their ardent idealism, diligence, and steadfast determination to help create a dignified future among their own kind, for the sake of their own future and for future

---

1. Prof. Joel E. Dimsdale, University of California San Diego, Department of Psychiatry
2. Immigration of Jews to Israel

generations. After all, so many other highly motivated Chalutzim did make it before them in the past.

However, comparing themselves with the difficulties of other pioneers, the survivors failed to take into account the most important factor in the equation, namely their own fresh, emotional injuries unlike any other kinds of insults, which they – every one of them – carried with them on their Aliyah.

In February 1957, when the last of the concentration camps closed its gates, the majority of the Jewish survivors chose to start a new chapter in their lives in Israel.

For those who decided to go back to Europe, the prognosis for their future seemed very gloomy; the American Jewish writer, Ludwig Lewisohn, predicted that

> those remaining Jews in Europe would live as 'outcasts, paupers, untouchables, in separate quarters of Europe' and lead 'a life without dignity, creativity, and hope'[3]

– which reminds us of Rabi Yochanan's famous statement:

> Since the Temple was destroyed, prophecy has been taken away from the prophets and given to fools and children . . .[4]

In any case, on May 14, 1948, the survivors heard Ben Gurion declaring Israel's independence:

> "*The Holocaust* which befell the Tribe of Israel in recent times, in which were led to slaughter millions of Jews in Europe, proved anew succinctly the necessity of a solution to the problem of the Jewish people lacking homeland and independence through the renewal of the Jewish state in the Land of Israel, which will open wide the gates of the homeland to every Jew and will grant the

---

3. Ludwig Lewisohn, novelist and translator was an outspoken critic of American Jewish assimilation.
4. Torah Tots/Jewish Press Midrash http://www.torahtots.com/jewishpress/20091113midrash.htm

Declaration of Independence Israel. Public Domain

Jewish people the stature of a nation of equal standing within the family of nations."

"The remainder of the refugees which was saved from the terrible Nazi slaughter in Europe and the Jews of other lands, did not waver from immigrating illegally to the Land of Israel in spite of every difficulty, obstacle and danger, and did not cease to demand *their right to live in dignity, freedom and honest labor in the homeland of their people."* . . .

This was history in the making!

The State of Israel

will be open to Jewish immigration and the ingathering of exiles;
will strive to develop the land for the benefit of all her inhabitants;
will be founded on the principles of freedom, justice and peace in the spirit of the visions of the Prophets of Israel;

May 14, 1948, Moshe Sharet signing the Proclamation of Independence

will implement equality of complete social and national rights for all her citizens without distinction between religion, race and gender;
will promise freedom of religion, conscience, language, education and culture;
will protect the religious places of all the religions; and
will be loyal to the principles of the declaration of the United Nations."

The survivors of the Shoah felt no longer like some pitiable victims of their time, but rather like having the supreme fortune of living at the time of the Redemption of Israel, when the age-old dream of the Jews has become fulfilled. They were about to re-establish themselves in their ancient homeland, to take part in shaping their own culture and the future of their own nation – all while building new towns and villages and making the deserts bloom.

This was probably one of the happiest moments in the lives of the survivors as future Israeli citizens – before some of the cruel facets of Reality started to hit them in their faces – and deep in their hearts.

Unfortunately, for many of those young optimistic Holocaust sur-

Hasenecke, Germany, November 1947, Dancing after the U.N's decision in favor of a Jewish state. Credit: Yad Vashem

vivors, life in Israel would turn into tragic old age spent in poverty and disgrace. Fifty years after the Proclamation of Independence, Israel would become

"worst place for Holocaust survivors",

some of whom were

"forced back to Germany due to Israel's lack of restitution laws."[5]

---

5. Ines Erlich, Israel News, 4.16.2007 "... Israel worst place for Holocaust survivors"

9 THE FIGHTERS FOR INDEPENDENCE

The number of immigrants during the entire Mandate period, legal and illegal alike, was approximately 480,000, close to 90% of them from Europe. The population of the Yishuv expanded to 650,000 by the time statehood was proclaimed.[1]

The limited number of veteran fighters from the Yeshuv – the Jewish population living in Eretz Israel – had obviously no chance to fighting off the Arab enemies alone during the 1947–8 war; the tens of thousands of immigrants who joined the army, known as GACHAL, i.e., Giyus Chutz La'aretz – Overseas Recruits – was therefore critical for winning Israel's War of Independence.

Ultimately, it is estimated that out of about 26,000 volunteers from Europe, ca 23,000 were holocaust survivors – there are no exact data available, just estimates from uncertain sources[2] – most of whom were drafted by the Zionist delegates who visited the German concentration camps soon after they were liberated from the Nazis.

---

1. The Jewish Virtual Library
2. "Israel's victory in its War of Independence war was determined to a great extent by the tens of thousands of young men and women recruited abroad in order to join the ranks of the locally born and raised fighters. Of the 26,000 recruits, 3,000 were Jewish volunteers from North African countries and international volunteers. The rest were Holocaust survivors." Dr. Hana Yablonka Ben-Gurion University From: "GACHAL Recruitment in the Diaspora."

Gachal Fighters, 1949, photo credit: "Amutat Dor Hapalmach"

It is therefore safe to assume that Israel won its Independence to a large extent thanks to Holocaust Survivors who chose to make Aliyah to Eretz Israel.

That, however, didn't do much to change the lowly social standing of those GACHAL-fighters, after they stayed in Israel in their capacity as new Olim. On the contrary: the sabra war heroes called the Holocaust Survivor fighters "GACHAL-yetz", to underscore the latter's weaker fighting skills compared to their own superior performances on the battle fields.

One of the few who appreciated the survivors' contribution to winning our independence was Ariel Sharon, who wrote in the article "The Real Heroes":

> These soldiers were foreign recruits (Gahal) commonly referred to as "Gahaleitzim" in a disdainful tone. There were no songs sung for them and no one conversed with them around the bonfire. . . . They had no one waiting at home with whom to share their experiences; they had no homes. They were people from another planet, with experiences that were alien to us, youngsters like ourselves but

hundreds of years older than we were. . . .

In Jerusalem's Mt. Herzl military cemetery, in the mass grave dug for our company, B Company, Battalion 32, Alexandroni Brigade, four of the 52 soldiers who fell in one battle were nameless.

(Fifty years later) "I particularly wish to thank all those unknown soldiers who survived the upheavals of the Holocaust a feat which required considerable bravery who dreamed of reaching safety and when they finally arrived once again took up arms in our defense. . . .

So many of them fell in battle. They, the Gahal soldiers, arrived unknown, fought unknown, fell unknown and many of them remained anonymous until today. In my mind, they were the real heroes.[3]

Arik Sharon

---

3. "The real heroes", Ariel Sharon, Jerusalem Post, April 24, 1998

10 "THE SURVIVOR SYNDROME"

To belittle Holocaust survivors is easy, because feelings of being inferior to others is, according to Dr .William G. Niederland,[1] one of the prominent characteristics of the "Holocaust Survivors' Syndrome." As a psychoanalyst who treated thousands of survivors of concentration camps and other catastrophes, he identified

> a severe sense of ongoing guilt related to the fact of their surviving while many others perished.

Survivor guilt is described in the Free Dictionary as:

> a deep feeling of guilt often experienced by those who have survived some catastrophe that took the lives of many others; derives in part from a feeling that they did not do enough to save the others who perished and in part from feelings of being unworthy relative to those who died.
> Survivor guilt was first noted in those who survived the Holocaust.[2]

---

1. Dr. William G. Niederland, the New York psychoanalyst, first described the "survivor syndrome" in 1961, based on his observation of patients who survived the Holocaust as well as natural disasters. Source: The New York Times Archives.
2. Free Dictionary, Survivor guilt

In his article "Shame, Guilt, and Anguish in Holocaust Survivor Testimony", Michael Nutkiewicz examines "how Holocaust survivors interpret the meaning of specific 'iconic,' all-absorbing memories that seldom find their way into the survivors' public account of their Holocaust experience."

Nutkiewicz postulates that

> . . . survivors live with countervailing pressures: the struggle to forget and remain silent and the need to tell and to memorialize.[3]

According to The Penguin Concise English Dictionary, "Guilt" is:

> **1.** the fact of having committed an offence, esp a crime.
> **2.** feelings of being at fault or to blame.

and "Shame" is:

> **1.** a painful emotion caused by consciousness of guilt, impropriety, or disgrace.
> **2a.** humiliating disgrace or disrepute; ignominy. 2b. a cause of disgrace.
> **3.** a cause of regret.

The Holocaust victims themselves are seldom aware of, or acknowledge, that they have feelings such as guilt or shame; in any case, most of the Israeli survivors prefer to hide their identity as survivors whenever possible.

---

3. Michaek Nutkiewicz, Shame, Guilt, and Anguish in Holocaust Survivor Testimony Oral History Review (2003) 30 (1)

11 WE ARE ALL EQUALS, EXCEPT...

We people are social animals, who are rating each other's relative importance according to hierarchies that we establish within our societies. These are social criteria that have been changing throughout history, according to circumstances that are developing in time and space.

In Europe, until modern times, the privileged classes were the various aristocracies that were passed on from father to son, regardless of talent or personal aptitude.

More recently, with increased social mobility, people could become educated and gain wealth and respect through talent and ambition within fields such as politics, business, science, art, etc.

In Eretz Israel, the earliest Chalutzim gained their respect through hard work and perseverance, and after a generation or two, according to seniority – being a native, or "Tzabar", a.k.a. "Sabra", Hebrew for Cactus:

> The cactus pear tree reached the Middle East several centuries ago. Its acclimation here in Israel was so successful that it became one of the distinct symbols of the land. . . .
>
> During the '30s and '40s, it served as a parallel nickname to "a Hebrew," and replaced it completely in the '50s. Beginning in the '30s but mainly in the '40s, the term transformed from derogatory to affectionate. The emphasis shifted from its outer thorns to its

inner, sweet fruit, to symbolize how the outer, masculine roughness covers, so to speak, a refined and sensitive soul.[1]

In our own time, being native, i.e., a "Tzabar" several generations back is among the highest marks of social status, which no amount of money can buy:

"7th generation in Israel" is the top of it all!

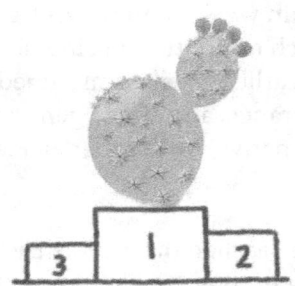

---

1. From, "The Chalutz and the Tzabar," Beit Berel בית ברל בית ברל הספר לאמנות המדרשה

12 COMMUNAL FARMS: A NEW WAVE OF STARTUPS

To paraphrase the famous slogan about women as a deprived minority:

> A Survivor has to work twice as hard to be half as appreciated as a Sabra

Every community has its own hierarchical social system; people who join any established society become strangers among the crowd, and they are expected to adapt to the locally accepted rules and social codes in order to get along.

In the established social system of Israel, the newcomer Holocaust survivors learned pretty quickly that the top of the social pyramid was taken by the brave, self-confident sabras.

On the surface, it appeared as if the newcomers had submitted to the "top-dog/under-dog" relation with the sabras, content with the humble status they were allotted. However, in reality, that wasn't the case: the survivors, on their side, thought that the sabras were snobs, usually arrogant, mostly emotionally constipated – to show one's emotions was a no-no in the sabra ethos – and often plainly rude; thus, the "new kids on the block" survivors asked: Were these boastful, self-appointed aristocrats not taught any table manners? Or to say "thank you" once in a while?

They seem to prefer spending time in groups (as part of "the herd

Photos taken of the young settlers of Kfar Daniel in 1949, private collection of Henia and Eliyahu Sela

Kfar Daniel's first settlers. Henia and Dr. Eliyahu Sela-Seldinger, Holocaust survivors from Rumania, were two of the Moshav's first settlers. Eliyahu (za"l) received his title Ph.D. in Philosophy, and eventually became the Director of the State School "Ir Ganim" in Kiriat Menahem, Jerusalem. He has published eight books, all from the periods Shoah and the establishment of Israel.

syndrome"), like sitting around a bonfire clapping hands (like certain tribes in Africa), singing songs that strongly resembled Russian folklore, often intercepted with loud cries of "HO-HO!"

Not surprisingly, although the survivors as new olim consented seemingly to their lowly social status among the veterans in the Yishuv, they felt more comfortable in the company of their own kind – in a kind of satellite social universe of their own.

Thus, the Holocaust survivors' strong motivation to stick to their own kind, which coincided with the urgent need for cultivating The Land, turned into a win-win situation: it gave birth to several new communal farms – the startups of those days. Hence, dozens of Moshavim (Farms) and Kibbutzim popped up all over the Yishuv within a short time.

Kfar Daniel was one of such cooperative farm (Moshav Shitufi) in the Modiin District, established in October 1949, named after Daniel Frisch, President of Zionist Organization of America (ZOA), who died in the year when the Moshav was founded.

A spade in one hand and a rifle in the other became the living symbol of this new brand of farmers, whose perseverance and determination "to build and to be built" was not just a slogan, but within a short time presented some genuine, visible accomplishments.

13 GERMANY OFFERS – ISRAEL ACCEPTS

To build is a costly enterprise; to build a whole country, such as the newly independent Israel with its meager budget, seemed like a mission impossible – until a unique chance to improve the country's finances appeared: it came in the form of West Germany's offer to compensate the victims of the Nazi regime, i.e., "Making Good" from German Wiedergutmachung –

> in a symbolic attempt to make up for the crimes committed by the Nazis during the Holocaust.

Constraints and opportunities

Each side had questions of gain versus loss, and money versus honor: Germany had to rebuild the country after its defeat in the war, while Israel had to build the country from scratch.

Germany's dilemma

The defeated Nazi Germany, that wanted to establish the German Federal Republic (popularly known as West Germany), was compelled to appeal to the victorious Allied Forces for permission; in

GERMANY OFFERS – ISRAEL ACCEPTS

DAVID BEN-GURION
ruled as Prime Minister

ELIEZER KAPLAN
Finance Minister

in Israel's 2nd Government
1 November 1950 – 8 October 1951

addition, the German nation had to admit its collective guilt during Hitler's ruling and pay compensation to the Jewish nation for it.

Those were painful conditions for being recognized as a sovereign state, but after the Germans decided to concede, Chancellor Konrad Adenauer delivered the following message in September 1951:

> In response to calls from Jewish organizations and the State of Israel . . . *unspeakable crimes* have been committed in the name of the German people, calling for *moral and material indemnity* . . . The Federal Government are prepared, jointly with representatives of Jewry and the State of Israel . . . to bring about a solution of the material indemnity problem, thus easing the way to the spiritual settlement of *infinite suffering*.[1]

Konrad Adenauer

---

1. From: Reparations Agreement between Israel and West Germany, Wikipedia

Menachem Begin with the sign that reads: "Our honor shall not be sold for money; our blood shall not be atoned by goods. We Shall wipe out the disgrace!"

Israel's dilemma

Germany's offer evoked a mighty dispute between Israel's leaders, some of whom objected to the very principle of accepting such a deal. Menachem Begin was fiercely against it.[2]

> Sons of Jerusalem, citizens of Israel. The most shameful event in the history of our people is about to take place this evening. At this bitter moment let us envision our holy fathers and butchered mothers and children who were lead in the millions to the slaughter by the Satan himself who arose from the bottom of hell to destroy our people . . .
>
> There was never in history anyone as cruel who dared to do such abominable acts in such proportions as the German murderers had done. . . . This was not just murder, it was incomparable brutal abuse and barbarity, a horror that the human tongue has no words to describe, unprecedented in history.

---

2. From: Reparations Agreement between Israel and West Germany, Wikipedia

But today, four years since the beginning of the redemption, a Jewish prime minister declares that he will go to Germany in order to get *money*, that for money he is going to sell the honor of the Jewish people and to impose upon it an eternal disgrace.

By contrast, Ben Gurion, who was worried about the impending financial collapse, including a severe food shortage, was very much in favor of the deal. In his diary, he wrote that the Finance Minister, Eliezer Kaplan, had informed him that:

David Ben Gurion

> the food situation is very bad. In another two months there will be no bread. Transportation takes 5–6 weeks. There is nowhere in Europe to get on credit. If we don't do something, there will be a tragedy.

The issue was brought up in the Knesset in early 1952, and after three days of arguments, a vote took place on January 6, 1952. A majority of 61 members voted in favor of authorizing the government to carry out negotiations with the Germans, while 50 opposed, 6 abstained, and 3 were absent.

Ben Gurion gave the freedom of ballot to the Holocaust survivor's representatives; however, he did this only after being sure that he had a majority supporting the decision anyways.[3]

Thus, on September 10, 1952, "The Luxemburg Agreement", a.k.a. "The Reparation Agreement" was signed by Adenauer and Moshe Sharett in the town hall of Luxembourg.

The Reparation Agreement stipulated that Germany would pay

---

3. From Wikipedia: Summary of the translation of "Reparations Agreement between Israel and West Germany." The text of the same chapter in Hebrew is:

"חופש ההצבעה ניתן רק לאחר שהתברר לבן-גוריון שקיים רוב התומך בהחלטה." ויקיפדיה, הסכם השילומים, גיבוש ההסכם

David Ben-Gurion — Prime Minister
Eliezer Kaplan, *Levi Eshkol* — Finance Ministers
ruled as in Israel's 3rd Government
8 October 1951 – 24 December 1952

the State of Israel, over a period of 12–14 years, a total of 3.45 billion German marks' (about $845 million) worth of merchandise, from which Israel will allocate 450 million marks to the Claims Committee: 30% of the total was transferred to England as payment for crude oil, and the rest was designated for the purchase of investments for the Israeli economy.

Parts of the Agreement were vaguely formulated, which were left open to several interpretations. By contrast, in the section concerning reparations to individual victims of the Holocaust, which Germany paid them for their *"infinite suffering"*, the position of Israel was very clear, and it was essentially different from all of the conditions accepted by other countries. That particular portion of the agreement leaned on the concept that it is *the State of Israel* that is the *heir of the Holocaust victims who perished* and left no surviving family.

Accordingly, all that Germany would pay in compensation should go directly to the Government of Israel, including that for the unspeakable crimes that have caused infinite suffering to the individual Holocaust survivors, such as forced labor, starvation, disease, etc., during Hitler's regime.

The Agreement was formulated in similar general terms concerning *"Jewish property"* that was stolen during World War II.

Thus, all of the three billion marks that West Germany paid to Israel during the next fourteen years, in what was called "material indemnity", went straight to the Israeli government.

Konrad Adenauer and Moshe Sharett sign The Luxemburg Agreement Communiqué Regarding Restitution for Israel and the Jews. From German History in Documents and Images (GHDI) Credits: Yad Vashem

Jerusalem railcar manufactured by Maschinenfabrik Esslingen, as part of the reparations agreement with Germany.

For the State of Israel this was a highly profitable deal:

> that money played a crucial role in establishing Israel's economy, and constituted a significant part of the national income, which in 1956, had reached 87.5%.

It is probably why our government decided to enact the "Disabled Veterans Act, 1954", which ensured that the survivors' money would go to the State Treasury permanently.

Notably, following the Luxemburg Agreement, each party was able to build its country rapidly: one thanks to the famous Jewish/Israeli talent for improvisation, and the other, thanks to the well-known German diligence.

Regarding the Israeli Holocaust survivors — what was to be their share in the Reparations Agreement with Germany?

Our politicians at the time decided that those penniless, severely traumatized individuals, for whom Germany's restitution would constitute a most significant material support, a veritable turning point in the beginning stage of their struggle to put their life back together — they of all Israel's citizens, should forfeit a considerable portion of their money for the sake of the country's continued flourishing.

Perhaps the most fitting answer, pertaining to our leadership's

management in that regard came from retired Judge Yaakov Bazak (see Chapter 22):

> (The State of) Israel made a bad deal in 1953.

It was a very "bad deal" indeed, with far-reaching consequences for the Holocaust survivors living in Israel.

Israel Ministry of Finance Jan 20, 2012 - From Wikimedia Commons.

14 A KIND OF PARTNERSHIP

The Zionist Holocaust survivors who made Aliyah soon after their liberation from the death camps enjoyed several privileges, among them:

- the right to volunteer to fight for Israel's Independence; and
- the right to stay in Israel

– although that cost them the better part of their German restitution.

As mentioned above, The State of Israel regards itself as the representative of the perished Holocaust victims; hence, in the "Reparation Agreement with Germny, the Israeli government demanded that *Germany should deliver its reparation to "the State of Israel" together with the Holocaust survivors' compensation* for their personal infinite suffering, which they endured during the Shoah, *in one and the same package* – with the understanding that the joint package of the two recipients would be separated, i.e., distributed to each group, at some later stage.

However, that later stage occurred only after the Agreement with the Germans had already been signed. Thus, by the time that a significant number of survivors learned Hebrew and would be able to claim their part of the reparations, the State had already taken over all the goods and money, most of which was invested in the country's infrastructure.

As to paying reparations to the survivors, our government decided to solve that problem by handing out allowances to them. This would be carried out according to certain criteria, i.e., depending on the kind and the duration of ordeals which the applicants claimed to have been exposed to during the Holocaust.

For this purpose, the Israeli Finance Ministry hired a special team of clerks, whom they qualified for evaluating the amount of allowances that the Holocaust survivors would deserve.

However, when it came to implementing the distribution to the survivors who lived in Israel, those specially qualified clerks came up against some difficult questions, such as:

- who should be considered a "Holocaust survivor"?
- how can "infinite suffering" or "horrific experiences" be *quantified*? and
- how can such phenomena be *defined* in the context of restitution?

Those questions went unanswered for many years to come, but our expert government agents went on with their task regardless.

To assure that the survivors deserved to be compensated for their alleged suffering, the specially qualified clerks would summon the applicants for a series of interviews, in order to familiarize themselves with as many details of every person's Holocaust experiences as possible. When those government agents became suspicious regarding the severe hardships that the survivors claimed to have endured, they felt obliged to interrogate the applicants several times in depth, since the amount of pensions – which eventually turned into charity, a.k.a. "government aid" – that the Finance Ministry would agree to accord them, depended solely on the interrogators' best judgments.

Ultimately, it was decided that our Holocaust survivors who came to Israel before 1953 would get about one-third of their German restitution, while the rest would become a part of the survivors' contribution to the establishment of the Homeland. Besides, argued the Keepers of the Treasury –

> The State has been burdened with financing the survivors' absorption into the country, so . . . .

Needless to say, the Holocaust survivors had come without any preconditions; as zealous Zionists, they would have come here anyway. Nevertheless, receiving all the restitution that Germany has accorded them could have helped the freshly traumatized survivors:

- to start a new life, particularly during the first years in the war-stricken Homeland
- to learn a profession
- to start a family
- to pursue some education
- to afford some leisure, beyond their daily struggle for their basic existence;

and in retrospect –

- even to save many of our by now elderly survivors from poverty, poor health, and despair, would they not have been forced to sacrifice most of their compensation to boost the prosperity of the country.[1]

As it turned out, the less idealistic survivors – those who chose not to make Aliyah, or to postpone it until after they recuperated somewhat personally and materially elsewhere in the world – they have by no

---

1. "Of the 193,000 Holocaust survivors living in Israel today, some 50,000 live in poverty." Lidar Grave-Lazi, Jerusalem Post, 23/04/2014

DAVID BEN-GURION — Prime Minister
LEVI ESHKOL — Finance Minister
ruled as
in Israel's 7th & 8th Governments
3 November 1955 – 17 December 1959

means become "outcasts, paupers, untouchables," as predicted for the non-Zionist survivors who failed to come to Eretz Israel right after the Holocaust. Actually, most of them are quite comfortable in their old age, supported by 100% of their German restitution ever since the mid 1950s.

15 THE EICHMANN TRIAL

Meet former Gestapo Colonel Adolf Eichmann

He was responsible for organizing and supervising the mass deportations, enslavement, starvation, and exterminations of millions of Jews in Europe.

After the fall of the Third Reich,[1] he fled to Argentina, and in 1960, after 15 years in hiding, he was kidnapped by Mossad[2] agents, taken to Israel, and brought to trial. Here in Israel, he was found guilty of 15 criminal charges, including crimes against the Jewish people, crimes against humanity, and war crimes, and was executed by hanging on May 31, 1962.

The trial sent a shockwave throughout the Israeli population as the people heard of all the horrors that the man behind the glass booth had planned and ordered to execute.

Many Israelis learned the details of the period called "Hashoah" for the first time. Some of those horrors were disclosed in detail both by the prosecutor, Gideon Hausner, and by over one hundred witnesses who had survived them just a few years before they moved to Israel.

---

1. "The Third Reich", Germany during the Nazi regime 1933–45.
2. The Mossad is the national intelligence agency of Israel.

Adolf Eichmann during his trial in Jerusalem

Many Israelis learned the enormity of what the name "Shoah" stands for, for the first time.

Abba Kovner, who warned Jews of impending doom as a 23-year-old in Ghetto Vilna, gave one of the most memorable testimonies at Adolf Eichmann's 1961 war crimes trial in Jerusalem.

DAVID BEN-GURION
Prime Minister

LEVI ESHKOL
Finance Minister

ruled as

in Israel's 9th & 10th Governments
17 December 1959 – 26 June 1963

Gideon Hausner　　　　　　　　Abba Kovner

Throughout the trial, many of the Holocaust survivors relapsed into acute states of post-trauma. Thousands began screaming during their recurring nightmares, many of them re-experiencing symptoms of the "survivor syndrome" after these had already submerged more or less below their waking consciousness.

Nathan Alterman, Israeli poet, playwright, journalist, and translator, wrote in an article called, "Concealment," in the Davar newspaper:

> We all knew that there were people walking among us from that world. We bumped into them every day in the streets, in the offices, in the stores, in the markets, at meetings. . . . But it seems that only during the course of such an awesome trial, the more that witnesses came up to the witness stand, the clearer the understanding was engraved into the consciousness of these survivors that they are an integral part of the essence of this living people.

Unfortunately, however, not even that "awesome trial" could change the attitude of our government toward our Holocaust survivors; they continued to deprive them of most of their German restitution.

In 2007, the State Comptroller, Judge Lindenstrauss, wrote in a "Critical Report Regarding Support for Holocaust Survivors":

> *Conscience cannot bear* that bureaucratic obstacles should prevent the proper treatment of these survivors who had passed through the seven chambers of hell during the terrible Holocaust that happened to the Jewish people.

THE EICHMANN TRIAL

LEVI ESHKOL — Prime Minister
ruled as
PINCHAS SAPIR — Finance Minister
in Israel's **11**th & **12**th Governments
26 June 1963 – 12 January 1966

However, the conscience of our decision makers at the top, who are directly responsible for the "bureaucratic obstacles (that) prevent the proper treatment of these survivors", seem to be unaffected by "the seven chambers of hell during the terrible Holocaust", which our survivors had passed through.

Nathan Alterman

As "public servants", they have exercised their cold, calculated attitude towards our Holocaust survivors for eight years before the Eichmann Trial, and they continued to do so after the trial, as part of their general "pragmatic approach."

Micha Lindenstrauss

16 LIFE IN TWO PARALLEL SOCIAL UNIVERSES

> "The least initial deviation from the truth is multiplied later a thousand-fold." Aristotle

The Jewish/Israeli ideals of modesty and the spirit of selfless service to "the people" were slowly, almost imperceptibly, shifting into a competition for materially advantageous policies and enterprises. This tendency has gradually split the Israeli society into "Haves" and "Have-nots": to Have was no longer embarrassing, and the social standing of the "financially comfortable" have become increasingly respectable; the power of bankers, contractors, and tycoons was steadily on the rise.

The victory of the Six Day War triggered an apparently latent neediness for possession – perhaps to make up for many years of austerity? – along with an unabashed race for power and riches, and a passion for abundance and luxury. Somewhat in the spirit of the businessman whom *The Little Prince* encountered in that very strange social universe on "The 4th Planet":[1]

> That man was so busy counting stars that he did not even raise his head at the little prince's arrival.

---

1. The Little Prince by Antoine de Saint-Exupéry. Summariezed by Y.F.

"Good morning," the little prince said to him, "Your cigarette has gone out."
"Three and two make five. Five and seven make twelve. . . . Phew! Then that makes five-hundred-and-one million, six-hundred-twenty-two-thousand, seven-hundred-thirty-one . . ."
"I have so much to do! I am concerned with matters of consequence."
". . . what do you do with five-hundred millions of stars?" – asked the little prince.
"It does me the good of making me rich."
"And what good does it to you to be rich?"
"It makes it possible for me to buy more stars, would any be discovered."

Tribute to the Little Prince, in Dniepropetrovsk. Image credit: Creative Commons.

The digression from the high moral values of the early days of our "chalutzim" signaled the dawn of a Parallel Social Universe – as if growing out of one fertilized egg that became divided into fraternal twins, each with a different DNA. Slowly but steadily, Modesty was OUT, and being Materially Well-off was IN. Diligence was no longer any prescription for respectability; rather, being successful meant: the more you own, the better.

Reversed Robinhoodism

Financially, Israel was already doing well, but The Disabled Veterans Act, 1954[2] was still in operation and our National Treasury still supplemented by about two-thirds of the Israeli Holocaust survivors' German restitutions. As The State was becoming stronger and

---

2. source: PsakDin.co.il

stronger, our Holocaust survivors got older and weaker, less and less capable of defending themselves against the all-powerful bureaucrats who were in control of their money.

Fortunately, the digression from the traditional moral codes and integrity that brought our nation back home from the Diaspora, is not the rule. Behind the noisy façade of our current diseased society, most, if not most, of our citizens, have never deviated from the moral principles of our country's chalutzim.

This positive face of our society is becoming most evident during international conflicts that erupt from time to time – including the Six Day War – when our national security, even our sovereignty,

is at risk. In such critical situations, our country is often rescued manily thanks to fearless acts and self-sacrifices performed by quiet, unpretentious citizens.

History teaches us that nature doesn't tolerate extreme imbalance of any kind for long. Thus, sooner or later, the present strange co-existence of life styles that are polar opposites, will have to be resolved into some more balanced social conditions – perhaps in style of "*The Emperor's New Clothes,*"[3] when an enlightened crowd decided to stop the game of fools and announced that

"His Excellency is naked!"

---

3. The Emperor's New Clothes, a short story by Hans Christian Andersen

17 ELECTION UPHEAVAL

The results of the elections for the 9th Knesset held in May 1977 ended the three decade long leadership by the "Mapai" working-class party and brought for the first time the right-wing "Likud" party into power.

Called the "election upheaval", it was considered to be the most influential election in Israel's history – a veritable political earthquake; by then a more mature democracy, it allowed the exposure of a series of corruptions by leaders of the former ruling party that often seemed to behave as if they were above the law.

Would such an earthquake in the new government's "democratic socio-economic" structure revoke, or at least ease, the decree of the Reparation Agreement of 1952 regarding the Holocaust survivors in Israel?

Dahlia Dorner

Would Israel's new government cancel the law enacted by the state's earliest rulers, which authorized to confiscate most of our survivors' Germany restitution?

Unfortunately, it did not.

Thirty-one years and seven governments after the "election upheaval," the State Commission, headed by retired Supreme Court judge Dahlia Dorner, was appointed to investigate the government's

handling of our survivors' reparation money.[1] Below are some of the commission's findings:

> ... the reparation money Germany has paid Israel adds up to *NIS 61.5 billion* according to current rates, whereas a mere *NIS 38 billion* have been paid to the survivors themselves to date.
> The 1952 Luxembourg Agreement stipulated that Germany would give Israel *$833 million* in money and merchandise, and

---

1. "Commission slams government treatment of Holocaust survivors", Amnon Meranda, 06.22.08, Ynet News.

Israel would look after the survivors, who would not be permitted to sue Germany directly.

State commission finds *individual survivors received NIS 1.3–2.2 million less than allocated*.

State Comptroller Micha Lindenstrauss' reaction to these findings:

this is not only a legal injustice, it is also a humane and public injustice.[2]

---

2. Anshel Pfeffer and Haaretz Correspondent, Jun. 22, 2008

18 LIVING WITH POST TRAUMA – POST *WHAT??*

Before "Shoah" became the common denomination for the Nazi genocide, Sir Winston Churchill called it:

> **a crime that has no name**

It took several years of research, debates and experience of experts to arrive at a more or less suitable diagnostic terminology for the special psychological conditions, which Holocaust survivors have in common. It is a highly complex mental/emotional condition that includes several conscious and/or unconscious, more or less identifiable features, and it tends to exacerbate in old age – to mention just a few of its characteristics. It most certainly appears as a result of severe trauma, hence popularly called *"Post-traumatic Stress Disorder".*

So, what is Post-traumatic Stress Disorder, or PTSD for short? One short answer is:

> *PTSD* **is a response by normal people to an abnormal situation.**[1]

---

1. The American Academy of Experts in Traumatic Stress

Sir Winston Churchill

A somewhat more detailed definition is:

> *Post-traumatic stress disorder (PTSD)* is a mental health condition that's triggered by a terrifying event — either experiencing it or witnessing it. Symptoms may include flashbacks, nightmares and severe anxiety, as well as uncontrollable thoughts about the event.[2]

QUESTION: How do PTSD sufferers cope in everyday life?

ANSWER: Experience shows that although many people who suffer from PTSD have adjusting and coping problems, these can often be overcome by taking care of oneself under favorable circumstances.

Unfortunately, that didn't work for the Israeli holocaust survivors; they were hardly in a position to take care of themselves having been exposed to one challenging situation after the other after they were liberated from the Nazis; the harsh conditions, which they repeatedly had to deal with, were often conducive to *Complex* PTSD –

---

2. Mayo Clinic

classified as "*A Syndrome in Survivors of Prolonged and Repeated Trauma.*"[3]

> Living with PTSD is one thing; living with it as Holocaust survivors in Israel is something else.

Another recommendation for coping with PDSD by expert psychologists was:

> Please keep sharing your experiences (for) dealing with PTSD.

This the survivors did after liberation "in the comfort of the 'Holocaust Survivors' Club" (see Chapter 5) as "residents" in post-war concentration camps, which took place in an atmosphere of mutual

---

3. Journal of Traumatic Stress, Vol. 5, No. 3, 1992

trust and understanding. However, with "Vatikei HaYishuv" (veterans of the Yishuv), sharing their experiences as former victims of the Shoah turned out not to be a good idea at all; most of the veteran Israelis simply refused to believe those people who claimed to have survived something that was "unprecedented in human history" . . .

In the early days of Independent Israel, the social universe of the "locally born & raised" Israelis was dominated by the ethos of stoic heroism; weakness was best hidden, preferably ignored. Thus, those who came out from the Holocaust alive were scorned for allowing the Nazis, first to chase them "Like sheep to the slaughter" and then to turn millions of them into soap – which is why the surviving "weaklings" were sometimes called "sabonim" (Soaps).[4]

Most of our survivors preferred therefore to keep themselves at some distance from their more "sturdy", uninvolved fellow countrymen, and to talk about their past only among their equals, i.e., other "Shoah-graduates".

Nevertheless, as time goes by, some people wonder:

Why did we keep quiet for so many years? Why didn't we talk? Why didn't we tell our story?

Why didn't we shout?

Ms. Devorah Weinstein's answer, which is true for many, if not most of the survivors in Israel:

> From the moment we reached the Land, we wanted to be like everyone – Sabras. Not to talk of our pains, not to complain, but to remain silent. So we changed our names, we spoke Hebrew, we forgot our mother tongue, we dressed in khaki clothes, we sang their songs, we danced their dances, all in order to be absorbed among them, to be like them.
>
> But it was all only superficial, while inside . . . .
>
> But now, friends, the time has come to talk, to tell, to write, to record.
>
> We are the last ones who can tell what it was like there. Soon, there will be no one left to tell.

---

4. Although it seems that the Germans did attempt to convert human fat tissue, especially from exterminated Jews, into soap, most historians believe that this did not take place on a large scale.

"A Soap" cemetery in Afula. Inscription on the monument says: "Here lies the holy ash collected soap and crematories"

So tell to your children, tell to your grandchildren, tell anyone who was not there, so that they will know and remember."
*Devorah Weinstein, member of YESH,
Organization for Children and Orphan Holocaust Survivors*

19 A MATTER OF PHRASING

Normally, when one party takes another party's property without permission, we call it STEALING – except in special cases in which it is politically incorrect to use the S word, or when disclosing the truth in real time is inconvenient for one reason or another.

Sometimes we encounter instances that fall into a grey zone between some action that may be considered pardonable although normally unacceptable; such complex cases are often debated and disputed in length – often so much in length until they ultimately fall into public oblivion.

One example of such normally unacceptable case appeared in a newspaper article, titled

> "Holocaust survivors' funds channeled to Israeli hospitals."

The reader is informed that:

Poriya Hospital near Tiberias will soon be getting a state-of-the-art underground hospitalization ward at a cost of $7.8 million. Some $1.2 million of the costs will be paid for by the Conference on Jewish Material Claims Against Germany (a.k.a. the Claims Conference),

Poriya Hospital, Wikimedia

the umbrella group that represents the Jewish people in negotiations for Holocaust compensation. . . .

Nearly $200 million intended for improving the lives of Holocaust survivors in Israel have gone in recent years to building hospital departments, old-age homes and nursing facilities. . . . while tens of thousands of Holocaust survivors are in need of help."[1]

There are numerous similar scandals, some of which are occasionally published in retrospect.

At the same time, hundreds of thousands of by now elderly and frail survivors learn more and more about the ways in which they have been betrayed, as a result of which they have to spend the last years of their lives in poverty and distress.

In his book "The Biological Solution", Raul Teitelbaum tells about

". . . the causes behind the scandal in which two-thirds of Holocaust survivors died without ever having received even one of the promised compensation payments."[2]

---

1. Amiram Barkat, Haaretz, Jul. 13, 2007
2. Raul Teitelbaum, "The Biological Solution" Book presentation 23.12.2008, Goethe-Institut Jerusalem

20 EVEN MORE HOLOCAUST ASSETS TO SHARE! –

The Absurd Becoming the Norm

In 1952, when the country was on the verge of financial collapse, Israel's rulers decided to seize most of our Holocaust survivors' German Compensation, which helped to rescue the country from bankruptcy.

Fortunately, since those difficult times, Israel has turned into one of the strongest economies in the West; yet, our government continues to confiscate most of our survivors' restitution, as did all our governments in the past. This means that Israel has got two kinds of taxpayers:

    a: those who are paying regular taxes, and

    b: those paying their regular taxes, plus a significant part of their German restitution, based on the Disabled Veterans Act of 1954.

"To 'The Jewish People' or to Holocaust Survivors – That is The Question"

> During the Holocaust years the Swiss banking community worked closely with many Nazis. Large quantities of pilfered gold and currency were deposited in Swiss banks. After the war most of this remained in Switzerland, as did money deposited by thousands of Jews from outside of Switzerland who had been murdered in the Holocaust.[1]

---

1. Switzerland – Yad Vashem Shoah Resource Center, The International School for Holocaust Studies

EVEN MORE HOLOCAUST ASSETS TO SHARE!

※※※

After the Swiss banks' associations with the Nazis had become uncovered, an international pressure on Swiss authorities led to the investigation into the whereabouts of the pre-war Jewish deposited fortunes.

The process of investigation, which became known as the "dormant Swiss bank accounts", started in the late 1990s. It developed into an ugly confrontation between two opponents: the Swiss, who were unwilling to give up the great wealth that came in their possession during WWII, and their various objectors, among them Israel, who reclaimed the Jewish assets, lost during the special circumstances of wartime.

- Would our survivors get this time a share of at least some of the Jewish wealth left behind, including the 6 tons of gold hidden in the cellars of the Swiss Banks?
- Not necessarily: Israel decided namely to lead the negotiations about the Swiss bank accounts via so called "government-associated" agencies, and, backed by prime minister Netanyahu,[2] they chose to refer to their claimants as *"The Jewish People"*.

Thus, like in the case of the "German Reparation Agreement", the term *"Jewish People"* allowed a broad range of interpretations, which enabled once again to exclude the people who have survived the Holocaust.

An even more recent development in our history of patronage over Holocaust assets was a draft proposition under yet another label, namely:

"The Fund for the Jewish People."[3]

---

2. see Chapter 21: Where Israel is failing the Jews, Marilyn Henry, September 23, 1999 Jerusalem Post
3. Keren Ha'am Ha'yehudi "קרן העם היהודי". Source: "Holocaust survivors oppose the establishment of The Fund for the Jewish People". Globes, 06/05/2001, Translated & summarized by Y.F.

This was initiated by Michael Melchior, former Minister of Social & Diaspora Affairs, described by some as "a leading advocate for social justice in Israel"[4] . . .

The proposition was presented by MK Avraham Hirchson,[5] at the time chairman of the Knesset's committee for compensation to Holocaust survivors, and it was supported by Mr. Avraham Burg[6] among other dignitaries.

The bill was opposed by all the organizations representing the Holocaust Survivors, as it became clear during the debate over the fund at the 15th Government's 270th meeting on January 16, 2002. That, however, didn't change anything in the matter.

Former Knesset Speaker Dov Shilansky remarked that "for years Israel robbed the survivors"; that the State's attitude towards our Holocaust survivors was unfair and humiliating and took the better part of the billions that were designated to them.

In any case, judging from past experience, any Holocaust related assets that might still be uncovered in the future are likely to fall in the hands of one "agent" or another, under one label or another, while our Holocaust survivors will be treated in similar unfair/humiliating manner.

Dov Shilansky

As to the Swiss and their banks, Gregg Rickman writes in his book Swiss Banks and Jewish Souls:[7]

> With the release of hundreds of incriminating documents, a dark side of Switzerland's democracy has been unveiled. Switzerland is now seen as a nation of greedy bankers, collaborators with the Nazis, and robbers of the wealth of the victims of the Holocaust.

---

4. "Jewish Agency opposes Melchior's plan for a `Jewish People's Fund'" Haaretz, Yair Sheleg, Jan. 14, 2002
5. Avraham Hirchson, a former minister; in 2009 sentenced to 5 years and 5 months in jail for stealing close to 2 million NSH from the National Workers Labor Federation, the Jewish Youth for Israel NGO.
6. Avraham Burg, former Chairman of the Jewish Agency and the World Zionist Organization, and Speaker of the Knesset.
7. "Swiss bank and Jewish souls" by Gregg J. Rickman, 1999

Rickman's book presents

> ... a powerfully enlightening account of how a small and determined group of people from divergent backgrounds humbled the legendary Swiss financial empire to achieve a measure of justice for Holocaust survivors and their heirs, while shattering the myth of Swiss wartime neutrality.[8]

---

8. Transaction Publishers, Apr 2, 1999

21 HALF A CENTURY LATER STILL HOSPITALIZED

Is this *"a land flowing with milk and honey"* **or** *"a land that devours its inhabitants"*?[1]

> The Holocaust inflicted intense, prolonged, repeated, cumulative, and unimaginably inhuman traumatic conditions on its victims. The Nazi bureaucratization of stress, trauma, and death-immersion experience was unprecedented in human history. Its colossal impact created a tremendous challenge to its victims' ability to make lifelong adjustments.[2]

Some of the most severely traumatized Holocaust survivors were incapable of starting a new life in Israel, so they were locked up in psychiatric hospitals. Many of them even remained there for the rest of their lives under the guardianship of Israel's Finance Ministry.[3]

Advocate Ronel Fisher visited one such psychiatric hospital, the

---

1. "The original expression, 'a land flowing with milk and honey', is a reference in the Hebrew Bible to the agricultural abundance of the Land of Israel. The phrase is used in the Book of Exodus during Moses' vision of the burning bush." Wikipedia
2. from: The Skewed Image of the Holocaust Survivor and the Vicissitudes of Psychological Research" Jacob Lomranz
3. Guardianship over Adults, http://www.jewishvirtuallibrary.org/jsource/judaica/ejud_0002_0002_0_01191.html

Abarbanel.[4] This took place after our country already had some impressive financial achievements, and building the country continued at an amazing speed.

Mr. Fisher witnessed firsthand some of the physical and mental manifestations of "stress, trauma, and death-immersion experience ... unprecedented in human history", which had driven these people to insanity.

The Germans, on their side, have been paying these fatally traumatized individuals accordingly; thus, all their money, saved during the past six decades, has made those victims virtual millionaires. That, however, had no influence on the extreme austerity imposed on the lives of the protected survivors at Abarbanel: Mr. Shmuel Zur, the state appointed guardian of those chronically tormented patients refused even to install air-conditioners in their rooms, on the pretext that

> it would be unfair to the rest of the inmates in the hospital.

Besides, those chronically traumatized people may not even notice the difference; their horrific memories from the past don't seem to change from one day to the next – they are fixed on events that they had experienced during the Shoah, so. . . .

In heart to heart talks with Holocaust survivors, Sara (psydonym), one of the patients at Abarbanel, told Chief Rabbi Lau: "I feel lonely, rejected by society".

The Chief Rabbi and Health Minister Yehoshua Matza, who visited the hospital following the publication of severe exploitation of helpless Holocaust survivors, were appalled by the heartless behavior of the Guardian General.

Yet, the English website of The Israeli Center for Legal Guardianship,[5] describes the institute as one that:

---

4. From Adv. Fisher's article in "Maariv", August 1998 "Shoah be Tashlumim" (Shoah in installments. Translated & summarized by Y.F.)
5. The Israeli Center for Legal Guardianship – The Fund for Care for Wards of the State – ". . . was established in 1977 as a nonprofit public trust by the Director-Gen-

> . . . provides professional, reliable, and compassionate services, with the utmost transparency and with a 'quality service delivery' approach,

where

> The wards' best interests are at the forefront of decisions made on their behalf. . . .

By contrast, the Hebrew website describes the services of the Guardianship in a way that is more likely to reflect the appalling conditions that have shocked the two above mentioned visitors.[6]

The following are a few excerpts from the Hebrew website:

- A person whose status is "Protected" is someone who is mentally or physically disabled and therefore needs someone to care for by guardians. Many of such people are Holocaust survivors living in Israel, and according to investigative reports published in recent years, many of them are severely neglected, often even robbed of their money, by their state-appointed guardians.
- Conflict of interests between the Guardian General and the protected is always there as a result of the very function of the Guardian General . . . The Guardian General has a distinct interest that the moneys of the protected should remain in its possession.
- In cases of protected who are financially well off, such as Holocaust survivors who receive compensation from Germany or disability benefits, the situation is even worse: if they get guardians who are unnecessary or unwanted, or taken advantage of and stealing their property, they have no legal right to take any legally valid action; they can ask to cancel the guardianship – but the courts usually refuse to accept such requests, especially by protected who are wealthy.

---

eral of the Ministry of Justice . . . The Center, as guardian, is oftentimes the sole body caring for those whom exploitation, neglect, and 'falling through the system' are conceivable situations given the characteristics of this vulnerable population."
6. אפוטרופוס Apotropus The Guardianship for the benefit of the protected in Israel http://www.apotropus.co.il

Amram Blum, who was the Administrator-General for 30 years, said:

> It is easier than robbing a bank.[7]

That is where our emotionally wounded survivors have been trapped, many of them since they came to Israel soon after they were liberated from the Shoah.

Professor Asa Kasher:[8]

> An honest person knows what to do with the funds of a childless, emotionally ill Holocaust survivor toward the end of his life. The State of Israel does not know. . . .
>
> It is difficult to say this, but there is no escape: The State looks like it is just waiting for the end of the lives of these helpless people so that it can finally take full possession of their fortunes and do with it whatever the people in the various offices decide to do. But even this is only the tip of the iceberg. Is it possible that behind this story there are other similar stories, all the stories of guardianship that the government provides for the helpless and childless, as if for their own good? . . . It is possible to do things differently, more ethically, more sensitively, more responsibly, that would appropriately benefit these mentally ill and childless survivors who deserve all the love, compassion and support that we can give them in their old age.

---

7. Mr Amram Blum, who was the Administrator-General for 30 years, said: "It is easier than robbing a bank." From Articles from newspapers (כתבות מהעיתונות) http://apotropus.co.il/media.htm

8. Asa Kasher, Professor Emeritus of Professional Ethics and Philosophy of Practice, and Professor Emeritus of Philosophy, Tel-Aviv University.

22 NEGOTIATIONS AND NEGOTIATORS

Most of this chapter is based on reports by Ms Marilyn Henry[1] concerning Holocaust related assets, hidden or confiscated, and about repeated incidents of profiting at the expense of the survivors of the Holocaust. Some of her articles mentioned below were published in the Jerusalem Post.

Holocaust assets amount to huge fortunes, which attract a growing number of both those who make profits at the expense of the survivors and those who are fighting against the injustice (see Chap. 1).

The first chunk of Holocaust related money became available with the German Reparation Agreement in 1952, which at the time was shared mainly between Israel and the Claims Conference, whose official roles was to administer compensation programs and distribute payments.

Since then, handling Holocaust assets has developed into a highly lucrative industry, involving a long list of activists, both private and public. Given the political and commercial interests at stake, it often creates scandals of undeserved profiting.[2]

---

1. "Marilyn Henry (March 5, 1953 – March 1, 2011) was an American author, columnist, journalist and historian and archivist for matters pertaining to Holocaust reparation, survivor benefits and art looted by the Nazis ... and a 'fierce advocate' for Holocaust survivors." Marilyn Henry, Wikipedia
2. From:"Where Israel is failing the Jews," Jerusalem Post, September 23, 1999 (Translated & summarized by Y.F.)

NEGOTIATIONS AND NEGOTIATORS 115

| Binjamin Netanyahu | Dan Meridor | Yakov Neeman | Binjamin Netanyahu | Meir Shitrit |

Prime Minister   ruled as   Finance Ministers
in Israel's 27th Government
18 June 1996 – 6 July 1981

> ... Israel did not want Holocaust politics to interfere with its diplomatic, economic and military ties with Europe.[3]

According to unofficial discussions, some of which have become exposed, Israel is caught between its position as the center of Jewish life and its national agenda: she doesn't want to let Holocaust interests interfere with its policy on Europe, but she also wants to keep its prominent role in significant Diaspora issues.

From one report by Ms. Henry, we learn that such was the case when Mr. Netanyahu (during his first office as prime minister), had to thank WJRO[4] for negotiating the over billion-dollar claims against the Swiss banks, but at the same time trying to assure Bern, that "Israel had no quarrel with the Swiss".

"The Holocaust is a hot topic", in Ms. Henry's words, and Jerusalem cannot ignore the issue of Nazi-looted property. However, it is obvious that Israel plays a passive role in retrieving lost assets during the Holocaust, compared to the energy invested in the topic by Jewish groups abroad.

This was clearly illustrated when Israel took part first in London in December 1997 on Nazi gold, and one year later in a US sponsored international conference on Holocaust-era looted assets in Washington; here, while the American delegation was led by US Secretary of State Madeleine Albright, Israel was represented by Avraham Hirschson

---

3. From:"Where Israel is failing the Jews," Jerusalem Post, September 23, 1999 (Translated & summarized by Y.F.)
4. World Jewish Restitution Organization

– at the time a Likud Knesset Member and chair of the Knesset's restitution committee – where it turned out that Mr. Hirschson came so ill prepared for his role at the conference that our delegation had to be reinforced by journalist Itamar Levine of Globes, who was an expert in the subject.

While Israel failed once again to provide the moral and political lead on unresolved issues of the Holocaust, as it was expected, the Israeli delegation declared in its official communiqué to the conference, that since the majority of survivors immigrated to Israel after the Shoah, and therefore they and their families constitute one-sixth of the world's Jewish population –

> The State of Israel, the Jewish state, sees itself as the central representative of *the survivors* and their offspring and is dedicated to achieving justice on their behalf and to *the remembrance* of the Holocaust.

The statement above did not specify how "The State of Israel, the Jewish state" plans to fulfill those important functions, i.e., serving the survivors as well as "the remembrance" of the Holocaust.

It did say

- that looted Holocaust property must be restituted, and
- that slave laborers must be compensated

all that, while

- Israel "supports and *recognizes the World Jewish Restitution Organization* as the umbrella organization, which works in close cooperation with *the State of Israel* to represent *the Jewish people* in matters of restitution".

Which begs the question, voiced by one American lawyer: "Since when does a government leave negotiations to a voluntary Jewish organization?"

※※※

Before the Washington conference, Netanyahu, who supported the legislation of the "Fund for the Jewish People, founded an inter-ministerial committee for planning a strategy on restitution.

The committee is supposed to allocate funds deriving from the Swiss banks and European insurers. However, there is almost no other information available about the fund, apart from a debate at the Knesset in January 2002[5], where the participants presented their arguments for the utility of the fund – mainly Deputy Foreign Minister Melchior – and others against it. In any case, well-informed sources don't have much faith in either the committee or the proposed legislation.

One Israeli diplomat remarked:

> There are many lawyers, Jewish organizations, and 'liberties taken by organizations in the name of the state', but 'no central authority on this in Israel.'
>
> For a while it was Burg,[6] then it was Hirschson for a while. It's a joke . . . The Jewish Agency has a role, the Finance Ministry has a role. The Justice Ministry has a meeting.
>
> Where is the Foreign Ministry?"
>
> It doesn't look good, not just for Israel, but for the Jewish people.

---

5. See Chapter 20, "Even More Holocaust Assets to Share!"
6. Avraham Burg, former head of the Jewish Agency

23 "... BUT WHAT ABOUT THE INDIVIDUALS?"

"Is the Government Unjustly Confiscating the Funds of the Holocaust Survivors?"

That was the question brought up on the TV program "Politica", with Mr. Yakov Achi Meir as moderator, broadcast on March 28, 1999.

This was one of the rare occasions when our government's attitude towards the individual Israeli holocaust survivors was discussed in an Israeli television program.

The debate took place among nine participants, all involved in the topic in one way or another.

The government chose not to send anyone to represent itself.

The argument was generally stormy, emotionally laden, and the answers to the central question largely reflected the various conflicting opinions of the issue, which ranged from

> "Yes, definitely!", "Yes, but . . . ,"
> and, "Absolutely not!"

In other words, all the way from accusing the government of robbing the survivors' money – which evoked a shocking reaction to the very use of the word "robbery" – to total support for the government's traditional attitude toward the funds of the Holocaust survivors.

The video, *"Jews against Jews, Holocaust survivors against the State of Israel,"* which was screened before the discussion, seemed to confirm the argument that the government indeed has been confiscating our survivors' money.

Naomi Porat, a journalist who came to Israel from Yugoslavia after her parents had been murdered when she was five years old and miraculously survived the Holocaust:

Yakov Achi Meir

> The injustice started from the original agreement between Ben Gurion and Chancellor Adenauer. . . . All the Israeli governments have received 200 million German marks each year, but only 30M was distributed to our survivors; and now when they are old and need money for false teeth, a wheel chair, etc. . . .
> Israel's governments have robbed the Holocaust survivors' money!
> "I have been fighting for decades with the various State-related institutions in an effort to change this situation with virtually no result.
> Avram Burg does today exactly the same thing. – Who has appointed him to represent me, my parents, all of the six million (who perished), and tour the world to collect money on our behalf?" she asked.

Mrs. Esther, as one of the few Jews to be spared from the executions that took place in the Soviet Union, came to Israel in 1974 with her two grown sons, because she wanted that they should live in their own country. She said that she feels humiliated and hurt by the law that deprives her right to get any personal reparations from the money that the Germans are paying the State of Israel for the survivors.

Yehudit Feuer:

> "When I came to Israel, I was shocked when I found out that the Holocaust survivors who came to Israel before 1953 receive only

about 1/3 of their German reparations, compared to survivors everywhere else in the world who receive their reparations from Germany directly to their private bank accounts – which obviously allows them a higher standard of living than the survivors in Israel.

Israeli survivors are discriminated against in their own country; they are treated as second-class citizens, deprived of their basic right to handle their own money, like minors or the mentally disturbed.

After these people managed to survive the Shoah, they chose to make Aliyah in order to finally live as equals among equals, only to find themselves financially cheated and humiliated in their own homeland.

Mr. Aryeh Barnea, a second generation Holocaust survivor, said,

Israel has accomplished one of the greatest transformations in history. However, it has forgotten several people along the way, especially the Holocaust survivors, who suffered more than any others. This may be caused by the development of the Zionist ethos in Israel, according to which only those who took up arms during the Holocaust deserve respect, in contrast to those who only passively survived it. Nevertheless, in a decision laid down by the Supreme Court, three judges spoke clearly:

"The financial rights of the survivors were withheld by the State of Israel."

(Y.F.: Among those who "only passively survived," were tens of thousands who responded to the call to come to Israel and take part in the War of Independence alongside the Israeli-born soldiers, and those who remained in Israel continued to fight in later wars as well. However, this too has been forgotten along the way. . . .)

The retired judge, Yaakov Bazak, who led an investigation into the condition of hospitalized Holocaust survivors said,

> One cannot say that the survivors were deprived by the State. More correctly put, we discovered that the State did not do enough for the mentally ill, for whom the State received and continues to receive reparations that could improve their living conditions, to give them something in their old age . . . some consolation, some pampering, after all the terrible suffering they have been through.

(Y. F.: It would be interesting to compare the judge's opinion with the testimony of Adv. Ronel Fisher cited in Ch. 21.)

> "But," said Judge Bazak, "We have to be realistic." The State of Israel made a bad deal in 1953. It seems that Ben Gurion, in his broad vision, did not imagine that there would be millions of Jews here, with tens of thousands of Holocaust survivors among them."

(Y. F.: oops! . . .)

Moderator:
> "But how do you explain, as a judge, the distorted reality that has persisted for all these years. Why has this law not been changed?!"

Judge Bazak:
> "I only wanted to explain that the money received from the Germans was adjusted to the standard of living that existed back then, to the wages we received. . . ."

Moderator:
> "Why are only the Holocaust survivors' reparations still adjusted to the standard of living back then?"

Judge Bazak:
"Yes, this definitely needs changing. . . . Regarding the above-mentioned money from Switzerland," said the judge, "If that 60 million was distributed among six thousand survivors, each one would only receive one thousand US dollars. How could that improve their situation? . . ."

Dr. Yechiam Weiss:
"This entire show, as if Israel is exploiting the survivors, is totally wrong. We have to remember the situation back then in 1952 . . . Without that money, it would have been impossible to absorb 1/4 million refugees. This money saved the State of Israel, saved its existence."

(Y.F.: oh, yes, that is very true; luckily, some Holocaust victims survived and made Aliyah just in time to save Israel's existence by their German restitution!)

Papo, the lawyer, whose steadfast opinion is that
"The State of Israel is the heir of the Jewish people who were annihilated. . . . and shame to those who use the derogatory expression "robbery" in that context . . .

Moderator:
"Are you referring to the Israeli governments that have been ruling, or are you overlooking the individuals involved?"

(Y.F.: Mr. Papo doesn't really care to answer that question)

Papo:
"The individuals who went through the Holocaust need certainly help, but . . . let there be no doubt, the State of Israel is *the ethical heir* and *rehabilitator of the Jewish Yishuv*."

Mr. Avram Burg, former head of the World Jewish Restitution Organization:
"We have to distinguish between two things. First, the question of the law enacted in 1953.
My problem with this deal is that it has persisted until today."

"... BUT WHAT ABOUT THE INDIVIDUALS?" 123

Mr. Burg used this opportunity to praise "the great contribution of MK Avraham Hirshenzon[1], former head of the Knesset Committee for the Restoration of Jewish Property, for his attempt to set right the injustice. Mr. Burg said he was pleased with "our" accomplishment in the struggle with the Swiss banks for the 60 million US dollars that were distributed "to those who suffered."

(Y.F.: "to those who suffered??")

"We distribute money in Eastern Europe and the rest of the world, but it is impossible to distribute it in Israel due to complex bureaucratic reasons *which cannot be overcome.*" . . .

The sole organization that exists for this purpose is the World Jewish Restitution Organization, which would have been able to distribute the money, but it is *the bureaucrats* who have been holding it up for over a year, and possibly *the politicians* as well; that may explain why the Treasury decided not to send any representative (to this panel)."

(Y.F.: As one who had been an influential politician and bureaucrat himself, Mr. Burg adds here an interesting perspective on organiza-

---

1. In September 2009, former MK Avraham Hirshenzon, later head of the National Workers Labor Federation began serving his five year and five month jail sentence for guilty of embezzlement of 1.8 million NIS and of money laundering, fraud, breach of trust, and falsifying corporate documents. According to the indictment, Hirshzon received the funds in envelopes that each contained 25–30,000 NIS in cash. Walla News, 16.01.2013 http://news.walla.co.il/?w=/10/2607315

tions, bureaucrats, and politicians, who are handling the survivors' money.)

Professor Moshe Zimmermann, who should have been the last participant in the discussion, could unfortunately not express his opinion before the program ended.

24 "MAKING HISTORIC AND SOCIAL JUSTICE" – INDEED!?

Over 60 years after Israel signed The Reparations Agreement with West Germany, the Governmental Advertising Agency of the Prime Minister's Office, in association with several other public offices, opened a campaign under the slogan:

"Making Historic and Social Justice." [1]

תכנית הסיוע הממשלתית לניצולי השואה
עושים צדק היסטורי וחברתי

The campaign was advertised in the newspapers, on the radio, on TV, on the internet, and a special, very attractive logo on top of the Prime Minister's Office's own website.

What happened? – asked our survivors:

- was our government undergoing some radical transformation in its attitude toward the Holocaust Survivors living in Israel? – or
- is the campaign even hinting at some historic and social *in-*justice that was done to our Holocaust survivors, which the government was about to admit in public? – or

---

1. Prime Minister's Office, the Governmental Advertising Agency, 2009

- could it even mean that our government decided to stop confiscating the lion's share of the survivors' reparations? – or
- has the government accepted the recommendation of "The Dorner Commission of Inquiry into Assistance to Holocaust Survivors" to pay the survivors a minimum of 75% of the funds that the Treasury has already received from Germany?[2] – or
- would our leaders at the top give high priority to the above mentioned committee's decision, since, in the words of State Comptroller Micha Lindenstrauss:

"this is not only a legal injustice, it is also a humane and public injustice"?

– Unfortunately, nothing of the sort.

So what was the campaign, called "historic and social justice", about?

It was about a few additional information centers, where our so called needy Holocaust survivors, by then most of them in their 70s & 80s, could find out about some minor benefits that were recently added to their meager allowances, such as: covering partly their false teeth and optical glasses, and allow certain rebates on some of their medications.

Unfortunately, most of our needy survivors (whatever such a status means) could still not afford such items, even after our leaders' "unprecedented" effort to bring about their "historic and social justice".

So, if our survivors asked at first: what happened? – after it became clear what the campaign, called "Making Historic and Social Justice", was about, they asked:

Is there no limit to our government's cynicism?!

---

2. "The Dorner Commission of Inquiry into Assistance to Holocaust Survivors published its report one month ago, in which it recommended increasing financial aid received by survivors who immigrated to Israel before the signing of the reparations agreement with Germany, to an amount equal to 75% of the aid received by survivors that immigrated to Israel after the deal was signed." Yael Branovsky, Ynetnews, August 5, 2008

25 WE WON'T FORGET

"The Holocaust struck mankind like an earthquake that no one can ignore. It destroyed one third of world Jewry, and the devastation it left behind is still haunting people ever since."

Professor Y. Lomranz [1]

Even the word "Holocaust" evokes powerful emotions, both among the millions of its victims and among the criminals who were responsible for it. It touches generations of nations and individuals, whether they are aware of what Holocaust represents or not.

Among the non-Jewish world population, we find different feelings and approaches to that immeasurable catastrophe, all the way from feelings of sympathy, through guilt or justification, to detestation. There are even people and nations who are denying that the Holocaust even happened.[2]

Jewish Communities worldwide are almost unanimously united in the effort to commemorate the colossal tragedy that shook the whole Jewish nation to its core. They help to build monuments, museums

---

1. The Skewed Image of the Holocaust Survivor and the Vicissitueds of Psychological Research, Jacob Lomranz,
2. BBC History, Denying the Holocaust, by Deborah Lipstadt

and libraries, collect documents and testimonies, and teach the Holocaust in schools and universities.

The State of Israel took on the leading role of safeguarding the memory of the Holocaust, as the disaster "unprecedented in human history", and this it does with remarkable devotion and generosity:[3]

> Yad Vashem in Jerusalem ". . . occupies more than 4,200 square meters . . . presents the story of the Shoah . . ."[4]
>
> The task of Yad Vashem is to perpetuate the memory and lessons of the Holocaust for future generations.[5]
>
> The Library of Yad Vashem is ". . . the world's most comprehensive collection of published material on the Holocaust, including over 125,000 titles in 54 languages, which is available to the reading public, safeguarding it for future generations"[6]

At the same time, Israel also took upon itself to distribute the Reparation Funds from Germany to its survivor citizens for their inhumane suffering. Sadly, our top decision makers are handling that specific aspect of the Holocaust with incomprehensible neglect, even sarcasm.

Israel's commemoration of the Holocaust is therefore, significant as it may be, a hugely biased investment:

On the one hand, the State is investing heavily in preserving the memory of the Holocaust, but on the other hand, it is consistently depriving our survivors for whom Holocaust is not just a symbol, Israelis who experienced firsthand

> the Nazi bureaucratization of stress, trauma, and death-immersion . . . unprecedented in human history[7]

---

3. Israel Ministry of Foreign Affairs. More than 30 heads of state and ministers from around the world will attend the historic inauguration of Yad Vashem's new Holocaust History Museum on March 15, 2005 under the patronage of the President of the State of Israel, Mr. Moshe Katsav and in the presence of world leaders.
4. Holocaust Museums & Memorials:Yad Vashem
5. Holocaust Museums & Memorials:Yad Vashem
6. Yad Vashem Library
7. The Skewed Image of the Holocaust Survivor and . . . Jacob Lomranz (2000), in "The skewed image of the Holocaust survivor and the vicissitudes of psychological research."

WE WON'T FORGET 129

ARIEL SHARON ruled as Prime Minister

BINJAMIN NETANYAHU EHUD OLMERT Finance Ministers

in Israel's 30th Government
28 February 2003 – 4 May 2006

∗∗∗

One of several outcries about the outrageous injustice toward Israel's survivors versus the grandiose cultivation of memorials, came from Retired Judge Dalia Dorner, who pleaded:

Invest in living survivors, not memorials.[8]

Mr. Zeev Factor, asks:

"What comes first, helping distressed people in the final stages of their lives, or investing in stones?" "Can't you commemorate the Holocaust with a few tens of millions less?"
"Did they have to cut through mountains in Jerusalem?"[9]

∗∗∗

"When the truth is inacceptable, it becomes the imagination of others" **Patrick White**[10]

---

8. Yael Barnovsky, Israel News 09.08.2008
9. from: Zeev Factor quotes
10. Patrick White 10, Nobel Prize for Literature, 1973

It is incomprehensible how these extreme opposite tendencies could continue for decades, until now, without any sign of change in attitude, let alone practice.

According to one theory, highly sensitive individuals cannot tolerate facing people who have been exposed to extreme suffering. That could possibly explain the perverted habit of ignoring or degrading our Holocaust survivors, who have gone through experiences that were "unimaginably inhuman." Even if such "allergic" individuals would stretch their imagination to the point of believing that some people did not die under such circumstances, they would need to protect their own fragile mental/emotional dispositions by placing such people at some distance from their own comfort zone.

※※※

There is another theory, one that may to some extent explain our decision makers' senseless investment in memorials, namely a cultural profile classification, developed by a group of social psychologists. It is based on the premise that

> "Time is defined as the past, present, and future,"

and that

> "Each culture values a different aspect of time."[11]

For example:

> "Past oriented cultures value tradition, ancestors, and family roots."

Judging from the high importance that Jews are inclined to attach to such values, we seem to belong to a predominantly past oriented culture – which may explain the present biased use of resources for

---

11. Cultural Profile, Time

preserving the past, on account of investing in necessities of the present.

Fortunately, that is now beginning to change, as our society, having recently become a multicultural immigrant society, is developing into a blend of time-related culture. For instance, we are gradually becoming a consumer society that appreciates instant gratification, which turns us into a more present oriented culture.

Then again, due to our prolific inventors of new technologies, we are increasingly oriented toward the *future* – something that is particularly fortunate, because

> "Future-oriented societies have a great deal of optimism about the future"

– in which case, we are also a *hope*-oriented culture (this is my own newly invented term, still unfamiliar to qualified social scientists), since optimism about the future is one of the prominent characteristics of the Jewish people. In fact, we have preserved our hope-centeredness throughout our long agony-charged history, while singing steadfastly our national hymn, focused on hope. Our national anthem "Hatikva", Song of hope, goes:

As long as deep inside	כֹּל עוֹד בַּלֵּבָב פְּנִימָה
Jewish soul longs	נֶפֶשׁ יְהוּדִי הוֹמִיָּה
And edges of the east	וּלְפַאֲתֵי מִזְרָח קָדִימָה
Eye to mark its viewers.	עַיִן לְצִיּוֹן צוֹפִיָּה.
Our hope is not lost	עוֹד לֹא אָבְדָה תִּקְוָתֵנוּ
Hope of two thousand years	הַתִּקְוָה בַּת שְׁנוֹת אַלְפַּיִם
Be a free in our country	לִהְיוֹת עַם חָפְשִׁי בְּאַרְצֵנוּ
The land of Zion and Jerusalem.	אֶרֶץ צִיּוֹן וִירוּשָׁלַיִם.

Our national anthem "Hatikva"   השיר הלאומי שלנו מתקווה
(Song of Hope)

Having already realized our hope to be free in our country, now, as a multicultural immigrant society, we hope to bring about Justice and Fairness in The land of Zion and Jerusalem.

26 WHY "HELPING OUR NEEDY HOLOCAUST SURVIVORS" IS A PROBLEM

INTRODUCTION

I. Progress with side effects

Young, idealistic leaders are prone to make many mistakes on their way to their idealistic goals, such as, in our own case, establishing an independent state.

One such grave mistake was to pick our Holocaust survivors as our country's rescuers from bankruptcy with most of their German restitution, and later, to add insult to injury, to keep our survivors as the country's permanent financiers, long after our economy had become established.

Meanwhile, we read:

"Holocaust Survivors' Welfare Fund threatened with closure"[1]

This was in the same year as the new Holocaust History Museum opened at Yad Vashem – "Crowning a multi-year redevelopment plan" – which cost nearly $100 million,[2] and two years later, when Israel was described as:

---

1. Ruth Sinai, Haaretz, Apr.07, 2005
2. Press Room, Yad Vashem 13 March 2005 New Holocaust History Museum to

(the) worst place for Holocaust survivors to live throughout Western world", and "Shoah survivors forced back to Germany due to Israel's lack of restitution laws.³

II. Post Trauma as time goes by

"The long-term after-effects of Holocaust traumatization are far-reaching. More than half a century after the war, the Holocaust continues to make its presence felt on survivor families and others in a variety of ways. Like an atom bomb that disperses its radioactive fallout in distant places, often a long time after the actual explosion, the Holocaust continues to contaminate everyone who was exposed to it in one way or another.

When retiring from work or experiencing deteriorating health, terrifying nightmares and flashbacks reappear in aging survivors who over the years had kept themselves excessively busy in order to repress their painful memories.

Survivors who were children during the war continue to struggle with their basic insecurities and prolonged mourning for parents they hardly or never knew."⁴

Regarding the later phase of *Post Trauma*, Prof. Haim Dasberg, M.D., explains:

"Chronic post-trauma illness, rather than gradually easing up with aging, is instead aggravated in numerous cases. This fact came as a surprise to many clinicians, so no wonder that late, belated, delayed or late-onset post-trauma reactions were not foreseen in the first two-three decades following the end of WWII in 1945."⁵

Open at Yad Vashem
3. Ines Ehrlich, Ynet, 16.4.2007
4. Natan P.F. Kellermann In: The Long-term Psychological Effects and Treatment of Holocaust Trauma
5. "Israeli society confronts trauma: The therapist vis-a-vis the survivor" HaimDasberg, 1987.

III. Further Consequences of the Israel-German Agreement

We often learn about our aging Holocaust survivors' growing problems and weaknesses.

Survivors are encouraged to share their experiences in the media as slaves, especially on Holocaust Memorial Day – which only helps to reinforce their public image as a miserable lot, who keep asking for help more than other aging citizens. We are rarely reminded of what we owe those survivors for all they did for this country.

Meanwhile, 60 years after Israel signed the Reparations Agreement with Germany, our present government, like all our former 32 governments, still shows no inclination to reverse the infamous decree that makes it legal to confiscate our survivors' money – which would certainly help them to help themselves.

So, why is helping our needy holocaust survivors such a problem?

There are several obstacles on the way to providing our survivors with the help they need.

However, even before attempting to decide HOW they could be helped, or WHO ought to help them, there is the problem of defining: who is a needy Holocaust Survivor?

A survivor in general is, according to Prof. Joel E. Dimsdale,

> ... one who has encountered, been exposed to, or witnessed death, and has himself or herself remained alive.⁶

A Holocaust survivor in particular is, according to Prof. Sergio Della-Pergola

> Any Jew who lived for any period of time in a country that was ruled by the Nazis or their allies is called a Holocaust survivor⁷

– in contrast to the more narrow definition of Professor Yehuda Bauer:⁸

> *Holocaust survivors* are only those people who . . . lived in ghettos and concentration camps or compulsory labor frameworks, who hid or who joined the partisan ranks.

Our own Finance Ministry is not committed to any definition of at all – although the office does keep a department, called the "Holocaust Survivors Rights Authority", which is

> in charge of implementing the laws regarding holocaust survivors, granting monthly payments, medical treatments, rehabilitation and welfare services.⁹

As already mentioned, one of several laws "regarding holocaust survivors" is "*The Disabled veterans Act, 1954*",¹⁰ which

> defines *the rights* of those recognized as disabled veterans (to) receive monthly compensation for disabilities caused by fighting against the Nazis

---

6. Joel E. Dimsdale, M.D. Editor Survivors, Victims, and Perpetrators: Essays on the Nazi Holocaust, Washington: Hemisphere Publishing Corp., 1984
7. Prof. Yehuda Bauer, one of the world's leading Holocaust researchers, Amiram Barkat Haaretz, Apr. 18, 2004
8. Yehuda Bauer, Historian of the Holocaust
9. from: Departments in the Ministry of Finance
10. The "Disabled veterans Act, 1954", from the website: "all right", "Page authorized by Holocaust Survivors Rights Authority" "1954 תשי"ד, נכי המלחמה בנאצים" "חוק נכי המלחמה בנאצים"

which, for some reason, at some point in the history of our Finance Ministry, became applied to the Israeli Holocaust survivors as well.

Given the lack of any agreed upon definition of the subjects under debate, i.e., needy Holocaust survivors, the argument around helping them seems rather pointless. The debate, however, continues regardless.

"Haaretz" reports:[11]

> Treasury and welfare officials are deeply divided on the handling of needy Holocaust survivors. Disputes at a special inter-ministerial committee revolve around: (1) . . . how much money should be distributed and (2) how to finance such measures.

The Treasury warns that

> . . . the broader definition of a survivor will overburden the state by billions of shekels. . . .

To be exact, the state would risk to be overburdened by what it has confiscated from our survivor' reparation money, that is to say, between NIS 1.3 to 2.2 million, which is what Germany has paid Israel for each survivor until 2007,[12] the year of The Dorner Commission's investigation.

To prevent such a terrible risk, our Treasury officials suggested

> increasing budgets for organizations that help needy survivors . . .

- The question is: which of all the numerous organizations that are appointed for the purpose?

> . . . and increasing old-age stipends . . .

- Here, the question is: by how much?

> . . . for the needy elderly.

- for WHO??

---

11. גורמים רשמיים ישראליים מתעמתים בעניין עזרה כלכלית לניצולי שואה הארץ, 11 במאי 2007.
12. "The Dorner Commission of Inquiry into Assistance to Holocaust Survivors" 2007.

Actually, if our Treasury would be willing to pay our survivors their due, it could use the definition

> *survivors of the ghettos and the concentration camps.*

Survivors defined as such have been compensated worldwide by the Germans ever since the mid 50s, i.e., right after they signed the Reparation Agreement with Israel; since those survivors are rarely needy at all, it is safe to assume that if our survivors would have received their due, they would not be needy either. In other words, if our Holocaust survivors would get their money back, they will no longer be needy, nor require any "help" from their debtors!

State Comptroller Micha Lindenstrauss wrote:

State Comptroller Micha Lindenstrauss.

> Israel's failure to legally define who should be eligible for survivor status has contributed to the delay in helping the survivors.[13]

Since our Treasury officials have been unable to find any solution to the problem of helping our needy survivors for several decades, many begin to suspect that

> Our Treasury (is) waiting for survivors to die[14]

which is indisputably the most practical solution to our state's problem with our needy survivors, especially as the number of Israel's survivors shrink by 35–40 every day.

---

13. Ynet reporters in Israel News, 15/8/2007
14. Raul Teitelbaum, "The Biological Solution"

27 THE SELECTIVE MEMORY OF THE SHOAH

Could our formal educational system be interested in deliberately hiding our Holocaust survivors' crucial role in the establishment and the building of The State of Israel?

Our survivors' important contribution to all the achievements of our fast progressing country is hard to ignore. Yet, in practice, this aspect of our recent history seems to be systematically kept in the dark, while the survivors are consistently presented as an aging, helpless lot, who burden our society with their constant neediness.

∗∗∗

In the summerof 2008, in an effort to improve the distorted image of our survivors, especially among the generations born after our independence, the Jerusalem branch of Amutat YESH[1] initiated a nationwide contest among high school students to write an essay on the subject:

> "The contribution of the Holocaust survivors to the establishment and the building of The State of Israel."[2]

---

1. YESH: Children and Orphans Holocaust Survivors in Israel (A.R.) (Amutat Yesh)
2. In Hebrew: "תרומת ניצולי השואה להקמתה ובנייתה של מדינת ישראל"

There would be 3 prizes granted to the best essays, the cost of which would be covered by the Amuta.

To participate in such a contest requires the Education Ministry's permission, in order to protect our children from any harmful influence by outsiders.

While applying for the required permission, the representatives of YESH were referred to a seemingly endless list of departments of the Education Ministry that are more or less related to Holocaust Education. In the end, we found a team, whose main task is to organize group travels to Auschwitz, who were willing to help.

Former Education Minister, Prof. Yuli Tamir, welcomed the initiative, but after she left her post, the invitations somehow didn't reach the schools; as a result, only a few students, who became informed by a devoted teacher in the South of Israel, took part in the contest.

After another three years of futile attempts to formally inform all our high school students, a secretary from the Education Ministry's office called to inform me personally that His Excellency, Education Minister Gideon Saar, is not interested in the contest.

The request to send Mr. Saar's message to Amutat YESH in writing was refused.

At about the same time, Mr. Saar was quoted in Haaretz:

> Israel will provide NIS 32 million for remodeling and preservation of the museum display at the Auschwitz-Birkenau death camp in

Poland. The commitment was announced yesterday by Education Minister Gideon Sa'ar at the cabinet's weekly meeting. 'Transmitting the memory of the Holocaust is a legacy to our people . . . 'The memory of the horrors of the Holocaust reinforces the significance of the establishment and existence of the State of Israel, the state of the Jews'.[3]

In early 2012, Mr. Natan Lavon, the director of Ken Lazaken[4], asked the Education MInistry's new Director General, Ms. Dalit Stauber, to reconsider allowing the contest to take place.

Hence, at a meeting on the 5th of February 2012, a second formal request was submitted to the Education Ministry. To date, beginning of 2015, the request has still not been answered.

In his article "The Erosion of Israeli Leadership," Isi Leibler wrote:[5]

> It is somewhat depressing to observe the stark contrasts between the caliber and extraordinary dedication of Israel's founding fathers and our more recent leaders. This would perhaps be understandable if we were now living in normal times. But alas that does not apply to our current situation. Despite incredible, even miraculous achievements at every level, the only country in the world still facing deadly ongoing existential threats from its neighbors cannot be described as normal.

---

3. Haaretz, Nir Hasson, May 2, 2011
4. "Yes! to Seniors" ("Ken LaZaken"), an organization that works to promote and improve the rights of senior citizens in Israel.
5. Israel Hayom, February 8, 2012

28 A PART OF OUR LEGACY

The *"dance macabre"* between our rulers' attitude of veneration toward the Holocaust itself, in sharp contrast to their consistent policy of demeaning those who have survived the Holocaust – and who then became our nation's most devoted associates-in-mission – has gone on practically from the beginning of Israel's recent history.

The politicians' motivation is obvious: they feel good about their generous spending for a worthy cause.

Our survivors' indulgence with our politicians' behavior is, however, baffling:

- why do they allow a handful of cynical bureaucrats to deceive them all these years?
- why don't they use the extraordinary powers that helped them to survive and then to come fight for Israel's independence?

This paradox – having exceptional capabilities accompanied by behaviors that are based on deep emotional wounds – is quite common among Holocaust survivors. It is one symptom of the survivor syndrome: people afflicted by it often have phenomenal strengths and courage alongside the trauma that they carry.

Some of that paradox may be explained by Victor Frankl's proposition that –

man's underlying motivator in life is a 'will to meaning,' even in the most difficult of circumstances.

According to Frankl,[1] the Austrian born psychiatrist and a Holocaust survivor himself:

> What man actually needs is not a tensionless state but rather the striving and struggling for some goal worthy of him. What he needs is not the discharge of tension at any cost, but the call of a potential meaning waiting to be fulfilled by him.

※※※

Israel's Holocaust survivors did their utmost to help establish and build our country, answering the call of a potential meaning waiting to be fulfilled. However, those same brave but severely traumatized individuals don't find the strength to turn against our rulers, who continue to cheat and humiliate them, and worst of all, prevent them from "forming their national identity" in their Homeland in full.

The question is:

How can such unethical policy be reconciled with the noble moral values of the chalutzim that dominated our society only a few decades ago?

The answer is:

It cannot.

However, just as the climate of extravagance and Narcissism has developed under extraordinary historic circumstances, chances are that further historic developments, along with the growing number of disenchanted citizens, will sooner or later pave the way to a healthier social climate, conducive to ideals more congruent with those engraved on the scroll of the Declaration of our Independence.

---

1. Victor Emil Frankl, "Man's Search for Meaning" (1992).

The State of Israel will...

- *Foster the development of the country for the benefit of all its inhabitants;*

- *It will be based on freedom, justice and peace as envisaged by the prophets of Israel;*

- *It will ensure complete equality of social and political rights to all its inhabitants irrespective of religion, race or sex...*

www.ingramcontent.com/pod-product-compliance
Lightning Source LLC
LaVergne TN
LVHW020933090426
835512LV00020B/3339